Build Bridges Not Walls

OVER THE PAST DECADE, the nature of business has changed beyond all expectation.

Advances in technology, changes in political philosophy, the blurring of boundaries between countries ... all have resulted in a more competitive and less compassionate world.

It's a world in which two-thirds of the people are working and the other third are looking for a job.

It's a climate in which competing jurisdictions in the same nation openly invade each other's territory in search of new business investment.

It's an environment in which unemployment assistance is being reduced, old people's benefits are being clawed back, social and health services are being slashed.

The duel for the dollar is relentless.

For the ordinary worker, with little say in such decisions, the effect is troubling. Increasingly alienated from the front office, uncertain of the future, the one on whom all production ultimately depends is the last person leaders and bosses turn to for suggestions.

This book seeks to reverse that situation. It offers decision makers some thoughts and ideas from the back office and the factory floor.

And it suggests ways in which bosses can survive with their essential humanity intact.

To: The Boss
From:
Your Employee,
Janet Andersen

Build Bridges Not Walls

A Wealth of Helpful Suggestions for Today's Business People-
Offered by an Outstanding Employee

"Janet Andersen's innate good nature shines through every line she writes in this employee's-eye-view of the contemporary business scene. Writing with wit and humor, she argues for a new style of business leadership appropriate to the Nineties. She calls for lean without the mean...for more vision in supervision...for the mutual respect between shop floor and the front office that has been lost in our rush to succeed."

Richard A.N. Bonnycastle, former Chairman, Harlequin Enterprises Ltd.

SPRINGBANK PUBLISHING
III

Published in 1994 by
Springbank Publishing
5425 Elbow Drive SW
Calgary, Alberta
T2V 1H7

First printing June 1994

Canadian Cataloguing in Publication Data
Andersen, Janet, 1952-
Build bridges, not walls

ISBN 1-895653-17-7

1. Personnel management.   2. Industrial relations.   I. Title
HF5549.A52 1994   658.3'145   C94-910501-5

Design: Catherine Garden Design
Production: DaSilva Graphics Ltd.

Printed and bound in Canada

This Is Janet Andersen...

ON IDEAS "We all have great ideas, but they're worthless if the energy isn't expended to make them happen."

ON PROBLEMS "Do you ever have those days when problems seem to follow you around? I used to go into the bathroom just to make sure I didn't have a sign on my forehead that said, 'PROBLEMS: CHECK HERE!'"

ON BUSINESS DIFFICULTIES "Companies are like people. They can be strengthened by adversity or they can let it destroy them."

ON RUMORS "Rumors have a propensity to grow big and fast. It would be wonderful if your money could compound as quickly as a rumor and take on so much interest."

ON OFFICE AFFAIRS "We have to take our hormones to the office with us, and they sure can cause a lot of problems! You have only to read 'Ann Landers' or 'Dear Abby' to realize that *office romance is alive and well and wreaking havoc.* I believe your willpower must be stronger than your passion power."

ON RIDICULE "When the workplace becomes a battleground for personal mud slinging, many brilliant ideas and careers are left in the dirt."

ON UNIONS "The first thing we must remember about unions is that *they don't usually choose their members.* Your business has control of the membership through the individuals it hires."

ON HIRING PERSONNEL "When you hire someone, do you look for a person who can speak three languages, but who can't say anything nice in any one of them?"

BUILD BRIDGES, NOT WALLS

Springbank Publishing
5425 Elbow Drive S.W., Calgary, AB T2V 1H7
FAX: (403) 640-9138

Acknowledgements

BUILD BRIDGES, NOT WALLS is a collection of observations resulting from my working life in the service industry. While these ideas are personal in origin, they cannot help but reflect the accumulated wisdom of all the people and companies who helped me along the way. In my various occupations—jobs which took me from the corner store to the service counter of one of the world's great airlines—I have benefited from contacts with innovative thinkers in all walks of life. I offer them all my gratitude. In particular, I acknowledge the support of Air Canada, a truly special corporation who, in my fourteen years of service, rewarded me with far more than a paycheck.

Some individual acknowledgments are in order. I particularly wish to thank Richard Bonnycastle who planted the seeds that created this manuscript. It was he who listened so kindly when I sought an outlet for my suggestions—and who suggested that I structure my thoughts in the form of a book. This is the outcome.

My thanks, too, to Henry Zimmer and Sue Blanchard of Springbank Publishing for helping me spread my message, to John Newton for his editing expertise, and to John Masters for his gifts of time, advice and gentle guidance.

Table Of Contents

The Jelly Bean Approach

THIS BOOK IS WRITTEN VERY DIFFERENTLY THAN MOST. It's not a textbook loaded with graphs and questionnaires, but a selection of random observations on business topics that you can read quickly and contemplate at your leisure. I think of it as my personal bowl of jelly beans—goodies I'm inviting you to share.

Why did I write it this way? First, because I find it the easiest way to express my ideas. Second, because I want you to be able to eat one jelly bean or several, but still get the flavor of the book. These days, there are so many demands on our time that it's hard to get past one chapter, let alone complete a book. So my jelly bean approach lets you take as much or as little as you like. Once you start, I'm hoping you'll become addicted and want to sample them all.

You'll notice the bowl has a wide assortment of jelly beans with a variety of colors and flavors. They're all mixed up but, as with our life experiences, the flavors don't blend together; each has its own unique taste. The book has no standard chapters and my ideas are random—so relax, and take your brain off cruise control. And, just as the colors and flavors of jelly beans repeat themselves, you'll find recurring themes in this book. *Repeating concepts and ideas helps the mind remember.*

How you eat my jelly beans is also important. You can eat them fast and not taste the jelly in the middle, or eat them so slowly that you forget there's a great variety. When jelly beans are eaten just right, you experience the subtlety of flavors; you may even wonder how to improve on the taste.

Again, don't read too quickly or go so slowly that you see only *words* without experiencing the concepts. I want you to *think* about my ideas. This is more important than liking the book.

Should you decide to throw out my jelly beans, all I ask is that you taste them first. Don't make an uninformed decision. Finally, whatever you do, please don't just save them for later. I don't want them sitting on a shelf. If you don't want my jelly beans, give them to someone who might. I didn't write this book to make money; I wrote it to encourage change.

I use metaphors or stories throughout because I think this is entertaining and fun. We often see a situation more clearly by comparing it with something not too close to ourselves.

Ideas Are Like Jelly Beans.
You Can Choose
The Familiar Flavor...
Or You Can Dare To
Try Something New

Great Bosses
Create Great People

GREAT BOSSES AREN'T BORN THAT WAY. Like leaders in any field, they consciously develop their skills. Moreover, most great bosses aren't exceptionally gifted; they don't have any secret formulas. In my experience, they're usually ordinary, comfortable people who are not at all intimidating. If they have any characteristics in common, they're probably a sense of humor, a love of other people, and an exceptional ability to communicate. Truly great bosses know exactly what they want from their staff, and set the example for others to follow. They have a vision and will go to great lengths to accomplish their objectives. They have a calm control about them and a way of guiding and inspiring others without force.

Great bosses ignite the spark that causes productive things to happen. The spark soon becomes a flame, and the flame a fire, creating the energy for success. Soon, they can stand back with little need to tend the blaze, as it gains the momentum to become independent. Yet great bosses are the first people to acknowledge that many other factors contribute to the fire of success. Their goal—*expressed as much by actions as words*—is mainly to be part of a winning team.

They possess a sense of fairness along with their strength. They will not be taken advantage of; neither will they take advantage of others.

Great bosses don't all work the same way. Their operating methods are often quite different because they set their own patterns, shaping the future to their own vision.

Great bosses rarely ask anyone to do anything they're not willing to do themselves. No job is too large or too small. But neither will they try to complete a major task alone, for they have learned not only how to delegate the workload but how an organization can benefit from shared responsibility. Great bosses don't aspire to be a one-person show. They have no desire for glory or acclamation. *They realize their own limitations and will ask advice and help when needed.*

Successful people generate warmth, have a closeness about them and tend to teach others to feel good about themselves. They bring out the best in those surrounding them. They are conscious of their own self-worth and don't need attention to feel fulfilled. They will be your friend, but not necessarily your buddy. They create respect for themselves and for everyone else— and they will work hard to maintain it.

Great bosses have faith in their employees' ability even when the staff themselves question it. Their honesty and faith create the fuel for that successful fire. They have the energy to forge ahead when most others have given up.

They act as teachers and expect others to learn and advance. Great bosses take pride in their employees' achievements and give them full credit. They'll set the stage, make the props, then let the staff create the play. At the conclusion, they'll lead a standing ovation, and show themselves to be their employees' biggest fans.

Great bosses provide the leadership that allows employees to say, *"We did it!"*

Great Bosses
Create Great People
Simply Because
They Believe in Them.

What Makes A Good Employee?

A GOOD EMPLOYEE IS:

1 honest
2 pleasant
3 hard-working
4 well-groomed
5 informed
6 mature
7 caring
8 independent
9 practical
10 creative
11 punctual
12 flexible
13 committed
14 his or her true self

A GOOD EMPLOYEE WILL:

1 look at work as a challenge, not a chore.
2 seek solutions, not find fault.
3 show pride in his or her self and the company.
4 want to learn new things.
5 be open to change.
6 perform his or her best every day.
7 ask "why?"
8 pity laziness, not envy it.
9 show appreciation of others.
10 take both the good and the bad in stride.
11 recognize his or her limitations.
12 never use others as tools for self-advancement.
13 work well both independently and in a group.
14 finish what is started.
15 admit to mistakes and learn from them.
16 have fun and keep a sense of humor.
17 feel equal to both peers and employers.
18 not let money be his or her sole motivation.
19 want to create a spirit of family.
20 know what level of contribution is expected.
21 have the knowledge to do the job right.
22 have a keen sense of fairness.

To Be A Good Boss, Just Replace The Word 'Employee' With The Word 'Boss'. The Same Characteristics Apply To Both.

Memo: From An Employee

To the Chief Executive Officer,
the Chairman of the Board,
and Company Shareholders

Re: Our mutual ambitions

This suggestion is written only because I care and I want to help. I don't wish to overstep my immediate superiors. However, since they cannot make the changes that are needed, I've decided to write directly to you.

You don't know me, but I work for you. I'm proud of the work I do and I take my job seriously. Like so many others in the company, I'm loyal and hard-working. You would never consider me a troublemaker, and I believe the work I do is important.

I wish there were a more effective way for us to communicate. Instead of a letter, memorandum or suggestion slip, it would be much more fruitful for us to talk face-to-face. I think we would understand each other better. I suspect we'd have much in common.

As I said, my job is important to me and I need to know if I'm serving the company well. I'd like to know if you take pride in the work I accomplish. I really want to be a member of a winning team, *but first I need to know the coach.*

On the surface, we might seem different. We may move in different circles, live different lifestyles, but our wants are the same. We both want to take pride in the quality of our product and services, and to feel we have something to do with our organization's success.

That's why I'm asking for the tools to do my job well. The

management people to whom I report must learn to be personable and communicative. So often, what *you* see in a manager is not what we see in that same person inside the workplace. *We need bosses who will motivate us by appreciating our talents.*

I realize that changes can't happen overnight, and I don't expect you to be a miracle worker. You, too, are only human, but that's the very side of you that I and my co-workers would like to see. We need to share our dreams and fears with each other, so we both don't end up feeling like strangers. Let's share in the challenge to create the best that is possible for our company.

Give Us The Tools
And We Will Finish The Job
Winston S. Churchill

A Smile: Nature's Gift

HOW MANY SMILES HAVE YOU RECEIVED TODAY? Or, a better question: how many smiles have you given? The number of smiles you give and receive will have a great deal to do with what kind of day you're having.

Some people believe a smile is little more than an upturned mouth. But a true smile is a whole wonderful expression. It's like a human light bulb being turned on. People instinctively know a true smile, and respond to it.

Nature gave us a great gift when she created the smile. In an instant, it lets us set the mood for a positive encounter. Smiles work wonders in calming nerves and building trust. They bring lightness to any situation. Warmth, understanding and caring are the result.

I saw a billboard not long ago that proved this point nicely. It showed a picture of a girl with an ear-to-ear grin captioned, "Give someone a facelift today." It reminded me of the "Happy Face" that was so popular in the 1970s. That big yellow face brightened the hearts of all the people who saw it. It was a huge success because it was simple, it conveyed a sense of caring, and was easy to understand. If a drawing can create so much goodwill, just think what *you* as a person can do!

A smile is one of nature's aids to a happier life—so make sure to use it often. And ask yourself: when you eventually get wrinkles (and trust me, it's inevitable!) wouldn't you rather have laugh lines than grouchy grooves? You betcha! After all, your entire attitude is reflected in your physical appearance.

Smiles are never factored into corporate budgets. Yet the more smiles your business gives and receives, the more likely it is that your business will prosper.

Smiling Is Good Business!

Me Or We?

SOME PEOPLE HAVE A WAY OF DANCING AROUND ISSUES and never taking a firm stand on anything. They spend their lives sitting on the fence, uncommitted to either side. They watch others do the work and make the decisions. It's as if they think they can fall into either camp at any time to reap the rewards.

Do you remember the tale about "The Little Red Hen?" The other animals played while she toiled away, baking bread. When the work was done, all the others showed up for a hand-out. I think it's time for a sequel to that story. In my version, the Little Red Hen shares her bread with the other animals, thinking they will appreciate all the hard work that went into making it. The wolf sits down and eats far more than his share but still complains about the way the grain was planted, how the flour could have been milled in a better way, how the bread is overcooked, and how the Little Red Hen didn't make enough for all his friends. The other animals agree, adding their own insults about the hen's performance. A squirrel joins the group and asks for a slice, but the wolf tells him it's *his* bread. The other animals are silent for fear that the wolf will target them for abuse. As night falls, a little rabbit thanks the hen for the bread and tells the squirrel the truth. The squirrel wakes the other animals and tells them how wrong they were, and how the Little Red Hen deserves their appreciation. Together, they chase the wolf from their midst. If this story were made into a play, could you be a member of the cast? And if so, which role would best suit you?

Do you suffer from the "opportunist" or "sponge" syndrome? Opportunists will always stay close to the action and air the opinions of the leader. They play the system for their personal advantage. Their only concern is winning the game, not playing fairly.

Spongers are people who merely repeat the ideas of others. They never express their own beliefs, but are like big sponges soaking up ideas and then squirting them back.

Standing up for what you believe in is one of the hardest things to do. The focus is placed on you, and your ideas become targets for criticism. You can expect to be laughed at, misquoted and misunderstood.

So why do it? Don't the negatives far outnumber the positives?

No! Taking a stand might cause you short-term problems but in the long run you come out the winner. Remember, *life isn't a dress rehearsal*. This play is ongoing and we must choose our roles wisely.

Many of the privileges we enjoy today resulted from the actions of strong individuals who stood up for their beliefs and who were willing to implement ideas and changes. They did the hard work and suffered the headaches needed to make a difference. They are the heroes.

The way we introduce change is also important. Don't force ideas on others; present your employees with new ideas and let them develop them. Most people fight change to some degree, so be prepared to be patient and understanding of their concerns. A friend of mine has a formula that summarizes human reaction to change: *30% will love it, 30% will hate it and 40% won't care.*

We can't all be leaders, but we can all work toward honesty and fairness. You can make a great deal of difference by setting an example for others to follow.

You Can Leave A Situation, But You Can Never Leave Yourself.

Create A Sense Of Belonging

AS HUMANS, WE LOVE TO BE PART OF A GROUP. I remember my anthropology teacher saying that over and over again. When we lose our sense of community, it creates a void in our lives. And this need for togetherness doesn't leave when people enter the workplace.

The strength of a business stems from the collective performance of its staff, not from the work of individuals running around in different directions. It's important, therefore, *to create a sense of belonging* for both employees and customers. If everyone in the operation is conscious of playing a vital role and can envision the development of something larger, they will all share a sense of pride and purpose.

A small boy stands outside a playground watching the other kids play ball. He would love to join them, but he hasn't been asked. The others think he's too small and won't be any good. He feels frustrated and sad, but doesn't ask to play for fear of being rejected. He begins to question his own ability. He feels like an outsider, and soon convinces himself that he didn't want to play anyway. However, unbeknown to himself or the others, he has exceptional innate ability. With practise and training he could have become a star player.

Instilling a sense of belonging in the workplace is easy if you encourage the creation of small groups in which employees can provide support and care for each other. Take steps to create a feeling of closeness within the unit and encourage employees to be there for each other's personal needs. Recognize occasions like birthdays and weddings, and show your sensitivity to such difficult situations as death, divorce and problems with children.

I can hear some of you saying, "I haven't got time for such things; I'm here to run a business, not a social club." This, despite the fact that, by showing personal concern for your employees, you can almost certainly expect an improvement in morale and productivity.

I know a woman who had given 25 years' service to a large corporation and was looking forward to her silver anniversary. The day arrived with a lovely pin and congratulations in the form of a letter from the district manager. The letter started with, "Dear *Mr. Employee*", and referred to *him* instead of her throughout. The spirit of this important day was lost forever. Blatant carelessness cost the company the loyalty of a faithful employee.

Most People Are Not Afraid Of Hard Work; They're Afraid Of Not Being Appreciated For It.

Getting Complaints—
And Enjoying Them!

WELCOME TO EVERYONE'S WORST NIGHTMARE: the IRATE customer or employee! When you least expect it, these characters appear out of nowhere and proceed to ruin the whole day. They raise your blood pressure, increase your stress level, and strain your nerves to breaking point.

Every business has its share of irate customers and staff. And since these unhappy individuals aren't going to disappear, it's up to us to learn how to deal with them.

No one likes a complainer, someone who constantly finds fault with everything. How can we ever satisfy such people? Yet we begin to do so when we realize that their chronic complaining is only a mask; the real problems are buried much deeper.

Faced with an irate person, try to become an impartial detective. Stay calm, and look beyond the surface. From words and gestures, angry face and closed body language, you'll find telling clues to some unresolved issues. The first thing to do is try to understand *why* that person is so unhappy. People often have good reason to be upset, and quite likely you would react in the same way if placed in their position. So learn to hear them out. If the complaint is reasonable, try to calm the individual and improve the situation in the best way possible.

Don't expect to solve things with a quick explanation— because everyone has a different interpretation of the facts. You'll need time, patience, and a willingness to listen. People need to feel a sense of importance. When they have a problem, they need someone to listen. Never be too quick to think you understand completely and cut them short, or dismiss their behavior as pettiness. Remember, a complaint signifies a real problem. What might seem petty to you might be of utmost importance to your employee or customer.

Communication skills differ greatly between individuals. In some instances, complaining is the only effective communication the complainer knows. The best way of dealing with these people is to guide them towards finding solutions to their *own* problems. They then start to move in a forward, positive direction, and a problem is no longer a problem if an answer can be found. Make sure to praise these people for any solutions they themselves offer. All ideas have merit and should be appreciated for what they are. If an idea is sound and workable, use it and give the individual full credit.

It's worth remembering, however, that not all complaints are reasonable. Sometimes, the angry individual is only using you as a sounding board for personal frustrations. Your complainer might be having a rotten day, and you, unluckily, have crossed his or her path. When this happens, don't lower yourself to the complainer's level, and try hard not to take it personally. A verbal battle will only make the situation worse. When you don't reinforce an angry outburst with your own input, the complainer's behavior will usually modify and the situation will lose its explosiveness.

If possible, try to isolate the complainer because this is a person who wants—and probably deserves—personal attention. If there is no audience, the noisy complainer will become quieter. Should a complainer try to intimidate you, be sure to hold your ground while remembering to be professional and polite.

Another difficult customer or staff member is of the 'cold shoulder' variety: the type of person who places a chilly distance between themselves and you. For these people, life is nothing more than a series of petty annoyances. Unfortunately, their icy attitudes have a way of cooling the warmest intentions.

During my high school years, I worked evenings and weekends at a local corner store. An older man came in every day to buy a newspaper. He had a habit of throwing his money on the counter. He would never speak a word or wait his turn in the line. One day, he came in, slapped his money down as usual, and picked up his newspaper. However, he had short-changed me because it was the weekend paper and it cost more. I caught his attention and told him about the extra charge. He started digging in his pockets, only to find he didn't have any more change. In frustration, he threw back the paper and started to leave. Since no other customers were present, I walked around the counter, picked up the paper and gave it to him. I told him I would throw in the extra dime if only he would smile. He started grinning and said, "Thank you."

As time went on, this gentleman became one of my favorite customers, and he would often come in just to chat. He eventually became friendly with the entire staff. One Christmas, my co-workers and I chipped in and bought him a scarf and glove set. He started to cry when we gave it to him. He had placed a wall around himself so he wouldn't be hurt. But once he started to trust, he became a wonderful, warm, human being.

Do you ever have those days when problems seem to follow you around? I used to go into the bathroom just to make sure I didn't have a sign on my forehead that said, "PROBLEMS: CHECK HERE!" It was always when I was tired and I didn't need the extra burden. Then one day I realized what was happening. On the days I was in a good mood, things tended to go well, but on the days I was in a bad mood…well, that's when trouble started!

The problem wasn't the job—it was me, and *my customers were mirroring my moods*. If I was short-tempered with them, they would react in the same way, and the people waiting behind them would sense it. The whole miserable situation would snow-ball. However, if I was cheerful and patient, they would respond accordingly. Conclusion: don't mirror your customers' or employees' unhappy moods. Try instead to have *them* mirror your *positive mood*. That way, you set your own working environment.

Problems Breed Problems! So Let's Try To Make Them An Endangered Species.

Three Key Words

SOME WORDS GRAB EVERYONE'S ATTENTION, and have strong impact on our lives. Three such expressions are S.O.S., DANGER, and HELP. They're attention-getting, highly important, and should never be taken lightly.

Business also has impactful words: words that can increase productivity, encourage self-esteem, build a caring employee group, and create happy customers. Yet, all too often, these words are overlooked only because they are so simple.

Three of these words were probably among the first we were ever taught. Our parents gave us some of the keys to success in our early years even if we didn't realize it at the time. *The importance of these words has not diminished now that we have reached maturity. If anything, they become more significant throughout our careers as we take on more responsibility and power.*

The first such word is PLEASE. We all remember our parents reminding us to use it. Children soon learn that they get their way more often with the magic word "please". We all-knowing adults, however, tend to question magic. Too often, when we use the word, we do so out of habit or formality, ignoring its persuasive power. It's like having Aladdin's lamp and being too lazy to polish it.

Consider, for instance, your own reaction to this magic word. Would you rather someone said, "Get the file," or, "Would you please get the file?" The order puts you on the defensive. The request enlists your cooperation.

The second word is THANK-YOU. People want to be acknowledged for a job well done, and "thank-you" creates that feeling of satisfaction. "Thank-you" is the universal expression of appreciation. By recognizing individual performance, it creates the spirit that accomplishes great things. We will work extremely hard for an appreciative leader.

Acknowledgment and appreciation create a domino effect. A person whose work is recognized is more likely to applaud other people's efforts. This process will not only continue in the workplace; it will also have a valuable impact on our personal lives.

When you fail to express your thanks, your employee believes his or her efforts are being taken for granted. That person will soon lose interest in the quality of the job.

The third word is SORRY. Many bosses find this the hardest one of all to say. Maybe it's because they don't want to admit to their mistakes. Or they believe John Wayne's line in the movie, *She Wore A Yellow Ribbon:* "Never apologize and never explain. It's a sign of weakness." After all, how can these corporate cowboys maintain their power if they own up to the fact they're only human? Errors can always be passed on to their employees, the economy or the competition, without reflecting on their own performance.

Bosses who pass the buck also pass on negative standards and examples. If you believe there's a stigma attached to the word 'sorry', your employees will be equally reluctant to use it. They'll try to bury their mistakes and productivity with suffer.

Unjust or miscalculated actions or behavior should not go unmentioned in business. We've all done things we regret, but which is best: to ignore our mistakes or to admit to them and make corrections? Fearful of tarnishing their perfect images, many companies and individuals would rather sweep everything under the rug. The problem with hiding the dirt is that, one day, someone will reveal it for all to see. Trust, once lost, is hard to regain.

'Sorry' is a word that expresses regret. It acknowledges that we did something inappropriate and that we regret it. But with that single word, we also have the means to correct our error—because the first step to rectifying a problem is admitting to it. *'Sorry' should not be an excuse; it should be part of the solution.*

Saying `Please', `Thank-You' And `Sorry' Is Not An Admission Of Weakness; It's A Demonstration Of Personal Strength.

The Past is Only That

THE PAST HAS A HABIT OF RE-ENTERING OUR LIVES. It is the foundation of our belief patterns. We all react differently to things because of past experiences.

Life isn't fair...nor is it on the level. There are many hills and valleys on the journey from the cradle to the rocking chair, and it's how we react to these that dictates our outlook. How well we respond to the challenges of this trip through time determines the quality of our life experience. Our lives would become very boring if we remained in a single emotional state, never having an opportunity to experience the peaks of joy or the depths of sorrow.

The past is probably the most important key to our future and success. In business, problems often have a way of being placed in File 13, in the hope they will just disappear. They're looked upon as failures that are best cast aside.

You would be wise, however, to examine negative situations and try to learn from such problems—for with understanding, they may eventually be solved. Similarly, a happy, positive situation should also be looked at to see what you or your company did to make the outcome so successful. That way, you can work toward duplicating the experience.

Making mistakes is all part of being human. Individuals who take risks are more likely to make mistakes, but these same people will live fuller lives because they realize *opportunity has a risk factor attached to it*. They have a resilience which helps them bounce back and learn from past misfortunes. A company that learns from its failures may ultimately reach the pinnacle of success.

Failure Is Only The Opportunity To More Intelligently Begin Again.
Henry Ford

Show Emotion

OVER THE LAST COUPLE OF GENERATIONS, it has become "not cool" to show too much emotion. Emotion is something we have been taught to outgrow. "Crying is for babies," "only cowards are afraid," and, "adults don't get excited." This stifling of natural reaction has dampened the human spirit and created a generation of plastic people. Our inability to express emotion has encouraged the use of artificial stimulants like drugs and alcohol and has contributed to nervous breakdowns and physical decline.

I remember reading an article in a women's magazine in the early 1970s that said you would never succeed if the boss ever saw you cry. I knew at that point I had better pack my bags, as I could never be at home in the halls of power. The fact is, I'm a very sensitive person and I feel other people's pain easily. For most of my life, I have viewed this as a personal liability and it wasn't until recently that I recognized sensitivity as a great asset.

Of course, to some extent, we must all learn to curb our emotions. Stamping our feet and crying over a cut finger is hardly acceptable behavior. But let's learn to *control* emotions, not *subdue* them completely. When we lower our guard and open up to others, the rewards far outweigh the disadvantages.

I'm always hearing about the so-called 'invisible space' around us—the six foot box we don't wish strangers to enter. But I believe this box exists only when we think someone *wants* something from us. It's a shield we erect for self-protection—but like any fence intended to keep others at their distance, *it also inhibits our own behavior.* My advice: leave the invisible space to the Invisible Man. The more trust you extend, the more you'll receive in return—and many of those strangers will become friends. I don't know how often I've reached over a counter and touched someone's arm. It has always seemed to calm them and take the stress out of a potentially explosive situation. *Don't be afraid to feel.*

I think we encourage people not to show emotion because it makes *us* feel uneasy. How often have you heard the phrase, "Don't cry"? But have you ever seen it do any good? People become isolated because we don't know how to react to them. Death, sickness, and sadness are all taboo subjects, so we often let others suffer in silence because it makes *us* feel better.

People don't like to touch because physical contact might have some sexual connotation. They think the other person might get the wrong idea and make too much of it. Obviously, the key here is moderation. You can't go around hugging and cuddling people for no reason. The action must fit the situation and touching is not a tool to misuse. Most times, all that's needed is a kind word or a smile.

This reminds me of something that happened when I was working as an airline representative. A passenger's flight had been mixed up and I rearranged his schedule so he could get home earlier. He was so happy he said, "I could kiss you!" I smiled and told him my husband wouldn't like that. He began to laugh and said his wife wouldn't be too fussy about it either!

The workplace needs a little excitement, so don't be afraid to show your enthusiasm. Positive emotions can create the energy necessary to develop wonderful things. Let business see the real YOU, a proud person with much to offer.

Don't Sell Yourself Short.
Let Them See Past The Plastic
Into Your Real Personality.

Awkward Feelings Are Normal

WANT TO KNOW WHO I TRULY ADMIRE? It's that godlike person who never gets flustered, stays neat as a pin all day long and enters every room with grace and poise. As someone who's more likely to spill cereal on my clothes at breakfast, or fall flat on my face while walking into a meeting room, I can't help but be impressed. Even my mother concedes that I'm clumsy—which is quite an admission for a mother. She used to tell me that I would outgrow it, which shows that mothers are not always right. I think it's because I never seem to do anything slowly. These days, my dreams of sophistication have long passed and I realize it doesn't matter how you enter the room, but what you do inside it once you're there.

We all have personal quirks we wish we could overcome, but we shouldn't let them stop us from doing things and accomplishing our goals. Personally, I wouldn't want to be perfect. Can you imagine how boring I would be?

Try to remember your first day on the job, how awkward and nervous you were. The other employees were strangers and you didn't know the daily routine or your role in it. Your sweat glands were working overtime, and your stress level was probably right off the scale. We're all placed in situations that cause uneasiness, but once we become familiar with our new roles, the anxiety goes away.

But what about all those people who—because they feel uncomfortable and vulnerable—*avoid* new situations and challenges? Aren't they locking the door to their own success?

My daughter Jenny is very talented musically, and when she was in Grade Four, her class performed the musical *H.M.S. Pinafore*. She was given one of the lead roles as *Buttercup* in which she had to sing several solos. On the night of the big performance,

I asked her if she had butterflies in her stomach. Jenny looked at me and said, "No, I have dinosaurs!" She couldn't eat her dinner and my heart went out to her. Nonetheless, she played the role and sang wonderfully that night, and we had a little family party to celebrate the occasion. That was four years ago, and last month she had to speak to her class about her proudest moment. She chose that night as her topic. Jenny had wanted to perform the role and had seen it through to the end. Had she surrendered to her nerves, she would never have enjoyed that sense of accomplishment. What a wonderful experience for a ten-year-old!

Now, let me share another story about my younger daughter, Carly. The summer she was learning to ride her bike, she decided to have a race with a friend. She lost control, flew over the handle bars, broke a front tooth, cut her lip, and was visibly scraped and bruised. Of course, we sped off to our doctor to find out if she had suffered any permanent damage. He took one look at her and asked, "Carly, are you going to ride your bike again?" She said, "Yeah!" and he smiled. He told Carly to slow down a little, practise a lot and be sure to wear a helmet. He knew he could fix the physical damage, but was more interested in heading off any emotional scars. When we arrived home, I told Carly she could miss school the next day and heal during the weekend. To which she responded, "The kids are going to have to see me Monday, so I might as well go to school tomorrow."

These last two paragraphs weren't written just to tell you about my family, but to serve as simple examples of how important it is not to let anything stop you from fulfilling your dreams.

It Isn't So Important To Win, But It Is Important To Try.

X-Ray The Problem
Before You Make The Cast

ONE DAY, WHEN LITTLE MARY WAS SKIING, she fell and hurt her arm. Her parents rushed her to the hospital to see what damage had been done. The doctor glanced at Mary's arm, then disappeared into an office with several other professionals. He returned to say that the arm was broken and needed a cast. He then went to work *placing the cast on the wrong arm,* never once asking the small girl where it hurt. Mary wasn't happy.

You are probably saying this could never happen. Most doctors know they must first X-ray an injured limb to determine the extent of the damage, then act accordingly.

But knowing isn't doing. In business, companies frequently proceed with solutions without first conducting a thorough examination of the *problem.* Unfortunately, the outcome can prove worse than the initial situation. Like the busy doctor, corporations sometimes expend their energies and financial resources in the wrong direction—then become frustrated at the lack of results.

Other businesses take what I call the Band-Aid approach. You cover up the sore spot with a Band-Aid and hope it will go away. Sometimes, this out-of-sight, out-of-mind solution even works...for a while. I've seen wonderfully creative Band-Aid programs that have provided valuable information and guidance for customers. But they rarely stay put. Employees are not willing to accept them because *the original problems have never been addressed.* These designer Band-Aids hide the problem for a while, *but the hurt will always resurface.*

My company once gave its employees a course intended to help us deal more efficiently with our customers. We were all taken off the job and placed in a classroom for several days. I particularly remember a morning spent discussing "open-ended" and "close-ended" questions. If you don't know what an "open-ended" question is, it's a question that can't be answered with a Yes or No. An "open-ended" question usually starts with a What, When or Why. A "close-ended" question can be answered with a Yes or No.

The discussion was informative but I never remember being impressed as a customer by someone asking me an "open-ended" or "close-ended" question. I do, however, remember occasions where people have smiled at me and shown friendliness. The original reason for the course was that we were extremely short-staffed and we could not spare extra time to talk with customers. But while this course was costing the company money, the original problem was magnified because the need for employees to attend the course made us even more short-staffed.

Energy is what creates change, but that energy must be focused in the right direction. Otherwise, it's as misdirected as someone walking backwards. Make sure you identify the right problem before finding a solution. Communication is the key, so be sure you understand your employees and customers before deciding what you think is best for them.

Solutions Are Best Found Together.

Little Changes Can Produce Big Results...

The way you hold this book and the way you read this page have suddenly changed. I did this to prove that *one simple change can make a great deal of difference*. The paper size, the lettering, everything remains the same except that the type is printed a different way. Sometimes, the most effective changes are the simplest.

At times, companies make the mistake of avoiding change because they believe a dollar value must be attached. They can't make any modifications unless they're in the corporate budgets. We've all heard the story about the child who gets the present his parents think he would like. He then sits down and plays with the box it came in, and throws the toy in the corner!

Feelings don't come with a price tag. Nicky, a very close friend of mine, is a nurse. Last year, she was told her unit would be closed down and that she would have to find another position in a different area of the hospital. This meant that Nicky would have to push a junior nurse out of work. The situation really bothered her, but since she herself needed the job, she moved over to the other ward, a unit looking after newborn babies and mothers.

The first day she was really nervous, wondering how the staff would accept her. She arrived for training to find that the manager had arranged a tea for her to meet the other nurses. The welcome was very warm and sincere and Nicky relaxed her guard immediately. Her new boss met with her, clarified what was expected from her in the new unit, and explained in turn what would be done for her. The first day set the mood for the development of mutual care and understanding. The unit now has a new employee who will go the extra mile for her peers and manager. Did this cost anything or even take much effort?

I saw a newspaper ad last Christmas that touched me. A company had taken out an ad thanking its staff for a successful year. Management acknowledged that profits were due to the performance of the employees. The customers were never mentioned, but I will always remember that ad, and take my business there. If they care that much for their own people, I'm sure the public is well-treated!

You Don't Need To Turn Yourself
Upside Down Or Sideways
To Make A Difference.

Don't Just Open The Doors—
Come On Out!

IN THE EIGHTIES, we heard a lot about the "open-door" policy. It was a first step in the right direction, but it seems to have stopped short. Now I think it's time for bosses to *really* open up their doors and show themselves.

With an "open-door" policy, any employee or customer can walk into the "big office," and talk directly to the person behind the mahogany desk. It's a bit like getting an audience with royalty. You enter their environment, and are graciously allowed to voice your suggestions or complaints.

While the idea is good in theory, it often doesn't work in practise. Usually, those involved are from different worlds, and can't understand, or don't want to understand, each other's needs. *Because they have never had time to build a trusting relationship with one another, the walls stay up...even when the doors are open.*

Face it: if your open door merely serves to make your employees uneasy, the policy isn't working.

One morning, I was going for coffee with a female co-worker, a person who had been working with our company for three or four years. We met our manager in the hall and I greeted him with a "Good morning." My co-worker turned to me and asked, "Who was that?" I said, "That's our boss!" This man claimed to have had an open-door policy.

The biggest asset a company has is its employees. Not knowing their needs and desires is like committing corporate suicide. As a boss, you can't expect employees to come to you; you must actively seek them out.

Try running more of your business from the work floor. You'll find it much more rewarding to see things first hand. And it's better to hear the news from those who are directly involved rather than getting the version that's been filtered through several levels of management. Too often, the main thrust of important information gets lost in translation. So have a coffee with your employee instead of issuing a memo. It's better business and it's much more enjoyable.

Deliver Your Messages
In Person.

Employee Support Is Your
Most Valuable Tool.
It's One You Must Constantly
Keep In Repair.

Hiring Employees

POSSIBLY THE MOST RESPONSIBLE GROUP of people within your business are those who recruit, interview and hire new employees. These people have the power to significantly strengthen or weaken your company.

When you hire someone, do you look for a person who can speak three languages, but who can't say anything nice in any one of them? Does a smile and a willingness to learn carry as much weight as an educational degree? Is experience more important than a positive personality? Education, training and past job performance are obviously important in the selection process, but these are *external* qualifications and I think more time should be given to the *internal* make-up of the individual. What *personality traits* does your applicant have that will enhance the company?

Education is obviously a strong qualification. It shows commitment to the learning process. It can also indicate the amount of interest a person has in a given area. But education doesn't stop when one leaves the classroom or when a degree is granted. It's an ongoing learning experience. Formal and practical education *together* help develop one's personality and outlook. Education is a key that helps unlock areas of individual interest. *A degree is not the end of a commitment; it is the beginning.* A résumé might chronicle impressive educational qualifications, but the person must be willing to transform that knowledge into creative, self-motivating and practical applications.

When you evaluate a prospective employee, past job performance is important because it reflects an applicant's reliability. Is work a serious undertaking to this person—or just a way to make a few dollars and move on? Businesses spend a lot of time, energy, and money training new employees, so recruits must be committed to learning and performing tasks faithfully. A new employee immediately becomes a representative of the company, and must be able to quickly adapt to his or her responsibilities.

Companies can gain a competitive edge if they hire a diverse group of people. Businesses whose employee base is limited to people of the same age, sex, ethnic, and cultural background have restricted vision! They see things only from their own viewpoint, missing factors of important concern to the general public. Your business will survive better in the global marketplace if you understand and respond to the legitimate wants and needs of others, regardless of origin.

I believe the workplace is a setting in which we can gain a better understanding of each other, one which will open the door to fairness and equality in all aspects of our lives.

One thing often overlooked by personnel officers is that, while they are evaluating an individual as a potential future employee, that same person is judging *them* as possible future employers. First impressions are lasting and each interviewer must be well groomed, pleasant, and easy to communicate with.

I once had a job interview with a gentleman who had the wrong application form in front of him and kept addressing me by the wrong name. He asked me questions like: Could I live off the salary they wanted to pay? Did my fiancee approve of me working? When was I going to have children? I finally asked him if he would like to see some letters of recommendation. "No," he replied, "because I have never read one that wasn't good." I walked out of his office shaking my head, wondering how this man could possibly choose future employees wisely.

Some of the best companies believe that selecting people is the most important single task performed by management. The more time and energy you devote to hiring personnel, the more likely you are to benefit from qualified, contributing people.

New Employees
Become the Company
In The Eyes Of
Customers And Clients.

Our World

THERE ARE OBVIOUS PARALLELS between the world of business and the natural world. Both relate to survival. In business, we're always reassessing our methods of operation. In daily life, we're constantly re-examining our relationship with the environment. When we talk about green preservation these days, we're not referring to our bank accounts. We're beginning to understand that if we continue to mistreat the earth, it won't be here to sustain future generations. We're realizing that we must invest in the earth's survival to counterbalance the neglect shown in the past.

While this book is not about ecology or environmental issues, the same principle of healing and rebirth applies to business. Concepts and ideas can be interchanged. The issues are different, but the same fundamentals apply. In every aspect of our lives, we must get back to basics, for no half-hearted solution can compensate for a lack of caring and genuine commitment.

Just as we must develop new respect for the environment, we must learn to nurture each other. It is time to care, not swear. This world is not a "man's world" or a "white world"; it is *our* world and it must be shared. I was brought up in the Fifties and Sixties in a middle-class, small-town environment. My friends were all from the same background. My daughters now go to school with people from around the world. When describing their classmates, they are more likely to refer to their haircuts than the color of their skin. With the advancement of travel and communications, the world is growing smaller every day.

Business can help us adjust to this new reality. From its wider perspective, it will comprehend that misunderstandings between peoples occur when we forget our common humanity...that closed minds and hearts invite dispute. By fostering understanding and acceptance, business will also benefit from the talents of a diverse group of people.

It's time to refocus. Let's learn to see our similarities and not concentrate on our differences. While we all want a say in the future, we must also be willing to listen to others. Leadership positions should be given to the most qualified individuals with no reservations as to their age, sex, race or creed.

There are conflicts and power struggles happening all around us in business. When bosses find it hard to give up control, it's not always because they are reluctant to yield authority. They're truly worried about what might happen. It's like giving your teenager the car for the first time. You might love and trust your kid, but you still have concern for his or her well-being—not to mention the vehicle! It takes time and patience for parents and teenager to become comfortable with this new situation.

It really bothers me to hear people find fault with others. Complaints and criticism come all too easily. Sure, the system isn't perfect, but it's the one we live by and we're all a part of it. By accepting responsibility, we can use our energy not to condemn others, but to make the system function more effectively. Pointing fingers only causes anger and misunderstanding.

We Must Learn To Work With People, Not Against Them.

Ask the Experts

THE STORES ARE FULL OF "HOW TO" BOOKS. Programs are constantly being set up to solve our problems, and we can find experts in every field willing to give advice. We can always place our burden on someone else's shoulders and have them propose solutions.

Much of the time, however, these books, programs and experts are providing information we already know. Their greatest benefit is in giving motivation, incentive and support. This book is a good example. I don't have unique solutions or guaranteed answers. I certainly don't offer any magic wands or secret formulas. I just encourage you to use your own head and follow your own heart.

Advice is a wonderful thing, but it's how we use it that makes the difference. Whatever the problem, it will remain yours and inevitably it will be you alone who finds the solution. By recognizing this, you can learn to respond to adversity and grow from the challenges that face you. Every business manager has problems and suffers disappointments. It is only those who overcome them who find success.

The owner of a beauty salon noticed that while her staff seemed to be working hard, their productivity was way down. She phoned the experts and they did a study to discover the nature of the problem. They informed her that the shop's lighting was poor and that the dark surroundings were responsible for the diminished performance. She paid them good money for the advice and closed the shop for renovations. Skylights were constructed, new track lighting was installed and she extended the front window. When her employees came back to work, they complimented her on the look of the new shop. However, as the weeks went on, the work level never improved.

Sometimes, the best experts to handle company problems are the people within your organization. They have a personal interest and understanding and can offer realistic solutions. No one has more interest in success than the person who benefits from it.

Given the opportunity to be heard, your employees will generate valuable input toward problem solving. They will appreciate the chance to contribute solutions to problems that affect them. Concerned employees have the real expertise most businesses are looking for and there is seldom a real need to seek professional advice in the yellow pages.

So are you still wondering why the employees at the beauty salon were working so slowly? *They all needed their scissors sharpened!* Communication with her employees would have saved the owner a lot of money.

If your employees contribute to solutions, make sure they benefit from the outcome. Reward the whole group by placing some of the savings into areas that will improve their workplace. Don't expect them to come up with workable plans on their own time. Don't give out "prizes" for the best idea. *Offering prizes is like buying an idea and suggests that you have no further obligation to the individual.* Personally acknowledge all suggestions and encourage personnel to take an active role in making their ideas a reality. You'll not only get answers to problems but you'll generate a sense of self-worth among your staff.

Often The Best Talent Is So Close That We Overlook It.

When You Teach Someone
To Walk,
Don't Show Them A Diagram
Of The Knee.
Show Them What There Is
To Walk To.

Janet Andersen

Training:
The Tool Of Advancement

OFTEN, WHEN TIMES GET TOUGH, the first expense a company will eliminate is the training department of its organization. The training function doesn't generate revenue so it's easily axed. In some minds, it's long been perceived as an extra—a bonus for the employees. But good managers realize that training and future advancement go hand in hand and cutting back is not the answer. Problems may not show up in the short term, but in the long run the company will fall behind.

If the mind is challenged and the brain kept active, cobwebs won't have a chance to form. Your employees will remain sharp and motivated to perform well. People are happier when they can see changes and opportunities for advancement within a business. They become more confident in their job performance, as they believe they have the tools to contribute to wise decision-making.

Through training and encouragement, you create multi-talented personalities who view life from a broader perspective. Your employees become more diversified in their outlook and gain a better understanding of the company's position, and that of other employees. The job won't become stagnant and interest levels will increase.

Ideas are like plants that must be given lots of sun and water. Great new concepts can blossom. Education stimulates the mind to become active and productive. Not only will the ideas you teach develop, but countless other interesting concepts will evolve. Each company sets the mood for its vision of the future.

Through the training process, you learn where different

people shine, what holds their interest, and what their strengths are. This helps you to place your employees into suitable, productive positions—and a winning team of happy individuals develops.

All of us need some guidance and training to reach our full potential. As individuals, we may have the brains, but intelligence cannot function unless fed by knowledge. A computer is useless until we input the proper data and the mind operates in the same way. The power might be there, but it must be harnessed properly to create the needed energy.

Training must be well planned. Programs are of no benefit if they are uninteresting, boring, or badly prepared. Employees will tune out anything they find repetitive or unrelated to their jobs. When teaching, remember not to put the cart before the horse.

Companies sometimes have a tendency to treat employees like schoolchildren when introducing new concepts. Employees are placed in a little room with pen, pencil and instructor. They are presented with the necessary information and are then tested to see how well they have done. The excitement level is about zero and the participants inevitably sit there waiting impatiently for recess (Oops! I should have said coffee break!). This process is demeaning to mature adults. They might not have the given knowledge, but they are not stupid and they need to be treated with respect.

I personally dislike role-playing as a part of such instruction because the whole idea is inherently phony. How can you react to a make-believe situation while real-life people sit around trying to find fault with your behavior? It's unnerving to say the least!

Hands-on experience is the answer. Let employees see how they can benefit from training. Give them opportunities to interject their own ideas, and contribute to the learning process. Sure, some information must be taught in a classroom but make sure it's done on a mature level.

Don't give a person a course once a year and think you have stimulated his or her mind for the next 364 days. Learning should be a natural part of the job; it should happen on a daily basis.

Don't let boredom and routine become your employees' greatest enemy. New ideas help the mind stay young and healthy.

Once We Stop Learning,
We Don't Live;
We Only Exist.

Employee Service Awards

THIS IS A SUBJECT OF GREAT INTEREST TO ME, and an area in which I have some personal insight and experience. I've won several service awards in my life, some as early as high school and others while working in a service industry. Accepting this recognition has given me great joy and has prompted many tears. In every case, these awards were presented with the best of intentions and caring. The organizations and people involved singled out my contributions in the traditional, time-honored way, and for that I say, "Thank you."

I do this, however, with some reservations. To my mind, there is a big problem with individually-given awards in that the presenter unconsciously differentiates between "winners" and "losers"—those who are recognized for their achievements and those who aren't. In business, the emphasis should be on the *team,* and *not* on single performers. If you want to create a family feeling, you don't show favorites or honor only high-profile personnel; you appreciate everyone for his or her contribution to the organization.

Frequently, the "winners" become the biggest losers in the reward process. They are identified as exemplary performers, and this can lead to loneliness and isolation. Even though they haven't sought the limelight, they find themselves in a fish bowl where every aspect of their performance is under constant scrutiny. Envy and jealousy commonly result.

Staff can also get mixed signals from rewards. Are they doing *their* tasks in the hope of a reward, or from a sense of loyalty and responsibility? Is superior service to be provided in a spirit of giving or for some ulterior motive? We should clearly understand that the act isn't half as important as the intent of the person doing it.

Service awards are certainly appropriate to recognize volunteer work but, in my opinion, they don't have a role in the workplace. Rewards given to volunteers often use the measurement of time as the major criterion. Sometimes, rewards are handed out for length of service because everyone is honored according to the same criteria. Businesses can also recognize the sales performance of people and give bonuses. Again, the rules of the game are the same for all. Service awards, on the other hand, can't be so easily categorized, because everyone's circumstances and situations differ greatly. There's no set standard to follow, and often the most helpful contributions are those made in private without anyone ever knowing.

Let me share with you the biggest reward I ever received in twenty-four years of working with the public.

Several years ago, my husband and I took our two daughters to Disneyland to visit Mickey Mouse and his friends. The girls and I were in a small shop in Los Angeles, when a total stranger came up to me and tapped me on the shoulder. He remembered me from the airline, and recalled that I had checked him and his wife in for a flight two years before. He told me they often spoke of that vacation and always mentioned me. Since I couldn't place the man or recall the situation, I thought there must have been some sort of problem for him to remember me so well. No, he said, there had not been any trouble; they had enjoyed a wonderful holiday, and I had been extremely kind and helpful in making it a success. I left the man with tears in my eyes because he had singled me out of the crowd in an entirely foreign place and situation. I had made an impact on someone without ever being aware, and had found out about it only through a chance meeting! No prize could have ever equaled that feeling. *This was an internal reward—far more meaningful than any public recognition.*

How then do you acknowledge outstanding performance?

Your employees expect their work to be appreciated and they value recognition above material rewards. *I believe that personal response is the most powerful way. This type of quiet recognition is direct, sincere and subtle. It doesn't only recognize performance, it centers on the individual. Employees feel special not only for what they do, but for who they are. Remember: people listen harder when you whisper than they do when you scream.*

I'm also a strong believer in the power of the pen. A "thank-you" letter is something a person can treasure and share. The time and energy a boss devotes to such personal communication is well spent. For your employees, it is concrete evidence of your appreciation. A phone call or a personal "thank-you," can also work but neither has such lasting impact.

Remember to acknowledge good work immediately. Don't wait days, weeks, or months to write your note because the effect will be lost.

Also, take the time to talk with these good employees. Find out what motivates them—and invite them to share their talents with the organization.

A famous painter once said that his greatest honor came when someone asked him to teach them to paint.

Recognize Those Who Give By Giving Them The Opportunity To Make A Difference.

Management:
The One We Call Boss

AS A BOSS, YOU'RE ALWAYS WALKING A TIGHTROPE. You must motivate and direct your employees while satisfying the demands of your business. You must balance the aspirations of your staff against the legitimate expectations of your shareholders. Knowing you have the power to generate profits for your company or to contribute to its demise is not an easy challenge. Are you prepared?

Ambition is a wonderful thing. It's what builds skyscrapers, creates new products, and finds solutions to the world's problems. Unfortunately, the word "ambition" also has a negative connotation because ambitious people tend to get a bad press. So, when we think of an ambitious person, we might imagine someone who steps on or over others for personal gain. Such individuals, of course, are not ambitious but *selfish*—and a smart boss will recognize the difference.

Many people are promoted as a result of effort, talent and loyalty. But there are also those who attain their positions by manipulation and dishonesty. They will unblushingly take credit for someone else's hard work. How can they do this? We all have aspirations, but surely there can be little satisfaction in achieving success at the expense of others.

When they are promoted, managers sometimes allow their new social and economic position to take precedence over their new responsibilities. Egos become inflated, and they begin to use their power for personal gain instead of the corporation's well-being. *A title is only as good as the person who has been given it.*

Please remember that you didn't gain more insight or intelligence with your last promotion, only more responsibility.

The brains didn't come *with* the job; you had to bring them *to* the job. What you say and do will have a considerable effect on how well your company is perceived by others. You are constantly under a magnifying glass.

Like it or not, leadership also demands that you be a mentor or teacher—someone who is there to serve the needs of others. It's a role you should take seriously. *After all, there would be no position for you if there were no employees to serve.* Use this opportunity to share your skills and knowledge wisely. Appreciate talent; don't be scared by it. Trust in the abilities of others. Remember, great leaders always use the strengths of the people around them.

As a boss, you are paid for the responsibilities of leadership, but everyone in the business is important. Like any team, it will only succeed through a unified effort. The better you know your employees and their strengths and weaknesses, the better you will do, and the more satisfaction your job will provide.

I don't believe for a minute that employees want to dislike their bosses. People appreciate guidance. However, if we believe that someone else is putting on airs or using the talents of others for personal gain, it is human nature to rebel.

Make Sure Your Power Has An Honest Purpose.

Pettiness, Politics
And Perks

THREE DOGS ARE IN SEARCH OF A BURIED BONE. The larger dogs' names are Politics and Perks, and the smallest is called Pettiness. They have their noses close to the ground as they try to smell out the juicy treat.

Perks darts ahead of Politics, and Politics shouts, "Stay behind me. Don't you know your place?" Pettiness thinks he might get his nose dirty, so he keeps his distance from the dirt. However, Pettiness thinks he smells something and tells the others. Politics again becomes angry and says, "Don't go over my head. I'm the biggest dog and it's up to *me* where we dig." Pettiness' feelings are hurt and he decides to go home and quit the search for the big bone. Politics and Perks sniff around the area, and finally dig in the very spot Pettiness had mentioned. Politics does all the digging. The dirt flies in every direction and finally, he cries, "Look what I found! Look what I found!" as he pulls up a large shiny bone. He drops the bone on the ground, panting hard to catch his breath. Quickly, Perks nips in, grabs it and runs away. Perks finds a hiding place and begins chewing on the bone as fast as he can. But his mouth is much too full. He gags on the bone and chokes to death! THE END.

The moral of the story is:
1   Pettiness can stop you from accomplishing your goals.
2   Politics often uses power instead of common sense.
3   Perks destroy; they do not enhance.
4   When you let pettiness, politics, and perks into the workplace, no one wins.

Self-Respect:
Don't Leave Home Without It

ACHIEVING SELF-RESPECT is an essential first step toward developing respect for others—because what we think of ourselves has a great deal to do with how well we treat our colleagues. In respecting other people as individuals, we must believe that we, too, have earned the right to be special and unique.

The important thing here is that we don't mistake self-importance for self-respect. At first glance, these characteristics appear similar— both describing people who seem sure of themselves and in control of their own situations. We have to look very closely to see the difference.

Consider a faucet of running water seen from a distance. You can't tell if it's hot or cold. You have to get closer to make that distinction. You must see steam or actually feel the water before judging. How you then deal with the water will depend on its temperature. In other words, the degree of heat dictates your behavior. If the water is very hot, you'll handle it much differently than if it is cold.

Self-important leaders have an exaggerated sense of their own importance. They exude superiority—hiding their human frailties under a mask of pomposity. These individuals place themselves on a pedestal and try to appear infallible—someone who is never wrong. As a result, they become alienated from the real world and lose touch with the people who inhabit it. To them, the ideas or interests of others hold no merit. Such people are more to be *pitied* than *feared* because they have closed themselves off from life, and their own self-importance is the key that locks the door.

Self-respect, on the other hand, is an *inward feeling of well-*

being, an understanding that oneself and everyone else are equally important. Self-respecting leaders are happy and content within themselves. They understand that all people have different ideas and interests, and they want to share and learn from them. They are prepared to give of themselves to experience personal growth. They are willing to take full responsibility for their own actions. They have gained an understanding of who they are and what they believe in. They are individuals who *open* doors—not lock them.

As a boss, you will benefit greatly from making a daily commitment to the ideal of respect. You can't rely on past performance, position or birthright. And it doesn't matter whether you wear a business suit or blue jeans. When you give respect, you will earn it from others.

"It Is Necessary
For The Happiness Of Man
That He Be Mentally Faithful
To Himself."
Thomas Paine

A BUSINESS FORMULA

Communication

X

$$\left(\frac{\text{Motivation}}{\text{Stimulation}} \right)$$

+

$$\Big(\text{Appreciation} + \text{Respect} \Big)$$

=

SUCCESS

Boredom:
An Infectious Virus

WE'VE ALL HEARD THE SAYING, "A change is as good as a rest". To keep our minds active, we must surround ourselves with new and interesting situations. Repetitive duties cause boredom, which in turn causes dissatisfaction. People constantly need to grow and change. Change stimulates the senses. Hence, we are only truly living when we are learning, for people merely exist if they have no challenges to meet.

Imagine what would happen if you took a group of eleven-year-old children and placed them in Grade Six for several years. In the first year, they would all experience new ideas and concepts and learning would be interesting. They would all probably gain some benefit from the time spent. In the second year, some of the work would become second nature, but most would still pick up ideas they had missed the year before. By the third year, however, the students would find it hard to concentrate on the subject matter, stop paying attention and start causing problems. In fact, by the time your students became teenagers—in their fourth year of Grade Six—you would probably have to enlist a second teacher to help control their behavior. In following years, the classroom would become increasingly chaotic and unmanageable.

Many companies have been doing the equivalent of placing their employees in Grade Six for many years. How then can they expect intelligent, healthy individuals to remain excited about their work? I've seen people work harder at getting *out* of doing work than at spending the actual time needed to complete their tasks. The challenge is to see how little one can accomplish while still keeping the job. These are not lazy people; they are too smart!

If you interest them in a new idea, they will give it their best performance. Remember: these same people will often leave work and go to the gym or run for miles, expecting no cash reward for their efforts.

You must recognize that boredom is a dangerous virus. When we let it take over in the workplace, it's not long before everyone starts complaining and finding fault with each other. Dissatisfaction, like a cold, has a way of spreading. Everyone, no matter how productive they've been previously, can become infected. If people aren't given challenges, they channel their thoughts into other outlets to keep their minds active. Sadly, much of this energy will be given to negativity and complaint.

I think that staff should be constantly challenged and given the opportunity to learn and upgrade skills throughout their careers. While this might cost a little more in training, employees will be continually more informed and perform from a much wider base of knowledge. Productivity and pride are byproducts of this type of action.

Employees need stimulation, so they can grow both personally and professionally throughout their careers. Businesses have a wonderful resource in their employees, but that power needs to be discovered, unleashed and then appreciated.

The Mind Needs To Work
To Stay Healthy.

Create A Feeling, Not A Program

BUSINESS IMPROVEMENT PROGRAMS are like television shows. They can be very educational and enjoyable, but for the people watching them, they are not real life. These observers remain detached; they are viewing someone else's ideas, created without their input. So when the switch goes off and the program disappears from the screen, they too are probably tuned out...or turned off. These same people, however, can develop strong opinions about a program, especially *if it's repeated.*

When an abstract situation has been developed by others, valuable information can often be overlooked as unimportant. This is especially true when program participants cannot relate or interject their personal views. They remain outsiders. The beginning, middle, and end have already been created.

If your program is to make a significant difference, it must *create emotion,* and show people how a concept or plan will benefit them *personally.* They must be given a role in the performance and share in the outcome of the finished product. Employees want to feel personally involved and to know their lifestyles will be changed by their actions. To achieve that involvement, you need to create a *feeling*—something that can't be taught, only conveyed by example.

You can't place people in a classroom with glossy photographs and manuals and expect them to leave with positive attitudes about themselves, the customers, or the company. Granted, they may leave with information and knowledge, both valuable tools in accomplishing a job, but *they also need motivation.* You must create desire, a feeling of want and an inner sense of importance. To make an impact, you must lead by example.

A program can come to an end but feelings do not. While feelings can change, they can't be erased from our minds. Feelings also have the power to grow while a program is usually much more limited in duration. Programs are driven by financial resources while feelings are fueled by emotion.

When you make a business plan, ask your employees how they feel about it while it is still in the formative stages. React to their responses with care and understanding. Take the initiative to break down barriers and walls, and you'll find that everyone else will do the same. Staff will only act in a cold and impersonal manner if they believe the company is cold and impersonal.

If water has been spilled on a floor, do you pick it up with waxed paper or paper toweling? The cost of both is about the same, and the energy to pull the rolls off the shelf is identical. So why does one work so much better on the mess than the other? The paper towel soaks up the moisture from the floor. It creates an open environment, thereby removing the problem. Waxed paper is neither porous nor open, so it repels the water. Similarly, if companies have a problem and want to enhance, enrich, empower, embrace, or inspire their people, they too must remain porous and open. It makes sense to match your response to the particular problem.

Feelings are the foundation of the company. They are what the public perceives and what sells your services or products. Warmth and caring go a long way in our cold computer-age world.

The Next Time You Communicate With Your Employees, Ask Yourself: "Did I Give Them The Right Feeling?"

Quality Or Quantity?

DO THE HOURS YOU SPEND on the job dictate the extent of your advancement and job promotion? Are you ready to give your soul to your job to achieve success? Does the quantity of hours equate to quality of production? Does one person working 80 hours a week equal two people working 40 hours a week?

The changing global economy has forced many companies to reduce their staff in recent years. Some businesses no longer ask but *demand* that employees devote some of their time off to work-related matters. One result is that *workaholics* are the norm, perceived as the only people who can compete in a global marketplace.

You and your employees must obviously be willing to go the extra mile, for the clockwatchers of the past won't have much of a place in the future. But how far is *too* far? Some people give too much away in time and emotional energy, failing to keep back enough for themselves. In attempting to generate higher productivity, all they produce is burnout. We don't expect our cars to run 18 hours a day without proper fuel and regular tuneups, so how can we expect anything more of people? Many individuals are running on empty. Are you?

The byproduct of workaholism is the creation of one-dimensional people. These are employees who live only for their work; they eat, sleep, and breathe the job. They have become obsessed, letting their jobs control them. The measurement of who they are is contained within their job title. *Their families suffer and relationships become secondary.* Their world becomes the job; they feel that, without it, they're nothing. Is that a good profile for a successful employee?

Our biggest concern should be ourselves and our personal growth and development. The more well-rounded we become, the more we have to give to others. Think of life as if it were a big picnic basket. We're all given a basket at birth, but the picnic we must create ourselves. Do you want to fill your basket with simple peanut butter sandwiches, or with food that takes more effort to prepare? Packing a varied assortment of meats, cheeses, breads and cakes will take more time, but it will make your meal much more satisfying. As a boss, you share the contents of your basket with others. When it offers worthwhile rewards, your employees will work enthusiastically to reach your mutual goal.

Today's smart bosses will loosen the reins a little and encourage people to pursue their own interests. Work plays an important role in our lives, but it's dangerous to let it rule our entire existence.

One-Dimensional People Miss Out In Our Multi-Dimensional Life.

Is It Time To Get Your Ears Checked?

DO YOU KNOW WHAT THAT PERSON JUST SAID TO YOU? Misunderstanding often begins simply from not properly hearing what someone is saying. Sometimes, we only hear a portion of a conversation, and take what we hear out of context. As a result, we may jump to conclusions—even become flustered, hurt or angry.

One day, I was working at the airport when an Oriental man came up to the counter and asked to purchase a ticket. I asked him where he would like to go and he said, "Away." I again asked where he wanted to go away to. "Away," he replied. I could now see I had a problem, so I explained that I didn't understand which flight he wanted. "I want to go Los Angeles," he said slowly, and then I realized he had been saying "L.A.", not "away". At the time, neither of us could understand what the other's problem was. I had thought he was being silly, and he'd probably thought I was being rude.

In retrospect, it's a funny story—but unfortunately, that's not always the case. Often, not hearing properly can ruin relationships and generate mistrust. We all hear and respond to information differently because of past experiences. If I mention "bungee jumping" to you, you might feel excitement because you want to try it. On the other hand, you might feel fear because it looks dangerous. If you're anything like me, you're more likely to think it's "crazy". Words induce feelings and sometimes suggest images that are quite opposite from those the speaker intended to portray.

If you have ever seen people interviewed after an accident, you may have wondered how they all could have seen the same thing, yet each have described it so differently. *The answer, of course, is that they all saw and heard the event from different angles.* Some concentrated on details, while others were caught up in the emotion of the situation. An accident, like any significant event, affects everyone differently. When the highlights are recalled the stories will vary.

Differences in perception are common in business. How the customer views your company can be the opposite of how the organization wishes to be seen. A C.E.O. will see things much differently than a manager or other employees. So be sure you're getting the right information, and think before you respond—because *words are irreversible.* I believe that, once spoken, they hang in the air forever. Misinformation persists. And hurt feelings can take a long time to repair.

Do you remember the childhood song, "Sticks and stones will break my bones but words will never harm me"? Only a kid could believe it. I believe words have destroyed more people than any other method of punishment. We can see the physical scars made by sticks and stones, but it's much harder to repair the emotional damage caused by unkind words.

Good bosses don't judge harshly—and they know that a little kindness goes a long way. So try to see the situation from the other person's point of view. Ask yourself: are you hearing what *you* want to hear…or what *someone else* is trying to tell you?

I heard a cute story that proves my point nicely. A man was traveling in the southern United States and found the city names very hard to pronounce. As he was having lunch in one of the local towns he asked his waitress, "How do you spell the name of this place?" She smiled and said "D-A-I-R-Y Q-U-E-E-N."

Poor Hearing Can Be Bad For Business.

Being Polite Is Not Enough

To Succeed In Business, You Must Be Polite To Your Customer: TRUE or FALSE?

I BELIEVE THE ANSWER IS BOTH TRUE *AND* FALSE. (There's nothing like a trick question to keep you on your toes!) It's true, because you can't succeed in business if you are rude and arrogant. That's like biting the hand that feeds you. If you think you are superior to the people you serve, they will sense it and become dissatisfied with your service or product. But the answer is also false, because *people want more than politeness.* Customers are looking for genuine care, a sense of importance and a feeling that their voices are being heard above the crowd.

It makes sense to be polite to people because politeness reflects the nature of your company and yourself. When you're contending with competitors selling similar goods and services, personal service can make all the difference between success and mere survival. In today's increasingly competitive marketplace, the quality of your service is more important than ever. You must look at everyone as an individual and be willing to give something of yourself to get business. You can't measure customers based on revenue, numbers or computer data alone. They must be considered as separate beings with special needs.

While I was working at the airline, a gentleman came to me early one day to select his seat and check his luggage for an international flight leaving much later. He handed me a handful of tickets. It was quite apparent he had been traveling for a long time and had covered a great distance. Since it wasn't busy, I asked him if he had had a chance to go up to Banff to experience some of the beautiful Canadian scenery. He told me he had been traveling for the past six weeks and had only seen cities from hotel rooms. I thought that was unfortunate and suggested that he might come back when he had more time. He left, but before long, I found him standing in front of my counter again. He said he wanted to thank me. When I asked why, he told me I was the first person in his six weeks of traveling to acknowledge him as a person. Others had been polite and had served his needs by getting him hotel rooms, meals and taxis, but no one had made the effort to *converse* with him.

People don't want to feel as if they're being treated like a thousand others. When you do that, no matter how un-intentionally, you're not adding to their day or letting them add to yours. Too often, we encounter other people and fail to connect, both parties sensing that the encounter is meaningless. It's rather like getting bulk mail. The message might be addressed to you, but you feel no emotional attachment to it.

Simple eye contact or asking a basic question will let others know you are listening and are responding to their needs. The rewarding thing is that you both become more satisfied, and the day is no longer a procession of empty faces.

Talk To People, Not At Them.

The Part-Time Dilemma

I WAS JUST WATCHING THE TV NEWS and the newscasters were discussing how the Nineties will see the emergence of a part-time workforce, with more and more companies giving employees reduced work hours.

I've worked part-time during much of my life. I started in high school and continued all through college. When my children were born, I again worked part-time, because it suited my personal needs. The difference between my situation and others, however, is that *I had a choice while many do not.* Unfortunately, full-time employment seems to be on the way out.

Many workers who have reached adulthood and taken on the responsibilities of a family during the last twenty years depend on two *full-time* salaries to maintain their lifestyle. For decades, they were almost guaranteed good jobs with 40-hour work weeks. Now, with permanent jobs being cut back to part-time situations, they find themselves forced to hold down two or more jobs just to get by. This not only taxes their strength but has a negative impact on their families and personal life. Businesses may flourish but families can be sadly affected by such a system. Is such instability necessary?

Another thing that upsets me about the concept of part-time employment is that many employers look on part-timers as "not quite" employees. It's perhaps the equivalent of *living* with someone versus being *married* to them. Part-time employees do the same work, require the same training, and should have the same commitment to the company as their full-time counterparts, but they are often looked upon as less important. Part-timers often get reduced benefits, particularly in health care and pensions, and are too often considered as mere "extras" by their peers.

If a change in working hours is inescapable, a change in employer attitudes is also inevitable. You'll be wise to try lessening the disruptive impact by taking your employees' personal situations into consideration when creating job-sharing positions. When you implement change, it's worth remembering that, *while part-time employees work a reduced number of hours, they do so without any reduction in feelings or brains.* Respect will go a long way towards resolving this issue.

A Part-Time Employee Is A Full-Time Person.

Live By Example

DO AS I SAY, NOT AS I DO. Many people live by this rule. They deceive themselves by finding fault with others instead of questioning their own behavior. They constantly complain about the junk in their neighbor's backyard without thinking about clearing out their own.

The obvious lesson for today's boss is to lead not by orders but by example. We all learn from the example of others, especially those we admire. Ideally, our leaders will demonstrate how we should respond to different situations. In the same way, we don't learn to love, care and show compassion from textbooks; we watch others and emulate their behavior.

Some bosses treat their employees with indifference. They don't want to get to know them or associate with them. It's not that the employees are treated badly; they're merely ignored. They have been hired to perform a task and that's all management expects from them. It could be that such a boss feels that to get too close could be dangerous. After all, he or she might, one day, have to let a person go—so it's necessary to maintain a certain distance and remain in control. This is like saying, "I never want to fall in love again because I might get hurt."

If you are unwilling to share yourself with staff, they will sense your reluctance and pull away from you.

Whether you realize it or not, you send out signals of what you expect from your employees. Do they, in turn, treat co-workers, customers and clients with similar indifference? It's far better to treat everyone with respect. Not only will you get that respect back, but your customers will respond to this positive atmosphere.

I once knew a prominent senior executive with a major company who was considered an outstanding role model. His daughter told me a story I have never forgotten, and the saddest thing is that she actually thought it was funny. When she was about six years old, she and her father were at a public outing when he accidentally passed some gas. He quickly turned to her and told her she shouldn't have done it. He was willing to blame his own child instead of accepting the humiliation himself. If he could do that to someone he loved, how would he treat his employees in a tough situation?

Honesty breeds honesty, indifference breeds indifference and mistrust breeds mistrust. Guidelines for business ethics should not come from a manual. They must come from the leaders who meet in the boardroom.

You Attract Not What You Want, But What You Are.

Procrastination:
Just A Big Word For Doing Nothing

WE ALL HAVE GREAT IDEAS, but they're worthless if the energy isn't expended to make them happen. Worse yet, some companies find it hard to make *any* decision without studying and reviewing a situation to death. It's a stultifying kind of overkill which didn't hurt when the competition moved just as slowly, but that's seldom the case in today's fast-paced economy.

Some bosses find decision-making difficult. Pretending to delegate, they find it easier to lay the burden on someone else's shoulders. Perhaps they fear making the wrong decision and being left to carry the blame. Others would rather spin their wheels than risk taking the wrong road.

Phrases like "looking into it" or "under review" sound very professional, but, in reality, they're a big cop-out. All situations need a certain amount of consideration, but most decisions should be made promptly. I once read that *successful people make decisions quickly and change their minds slowly,* and I believe that statement holds true. The best decision-makers rely on their experience, personal judgment, and sixth sense to help them come to conclusions. They realize *opportunities are made* and don't just happen.

I often wonder if Alexander Graham Bell would have invented the telephone if he had "studied the impact first", or if Christopher Columbus did "a feasibility study" on the possibility of discovering America instead of the Indies.

We all procrastinate over certain things. I personally hate the chore of washing windows and can always think of a million excuses to avoid it. The funny thing is that once I start the job, it isn't half as bad as I'd figured. I've blown the whole thing out of proportion. Sometimes, we expend more energy thinking about a task than we do in following it through.

If tomorrow never comes, the opportunities of today will be lost forever.

You Might Be On The Right Track, But If You Stand Still, You'll Be Run Over.

What Do You Mean, S*T*R*E*S*S!!!!!?

LONG GONE ARE THE DAYS when letting out the cows in the morning and making sure you had enough wood for the fire were your major concerns. Today, we have wonderful conveniences to make life easier, but that old bugbear *stress* is more prevalent than ever.

Stress can be most productive if effectively harnessed. If we had no stress in our lives, very little would ever get done. We would have no time restrictions and life would offer no challenges. Stress helps stimulate the mind; it delineates boundaries and gives us standards to work from.

The amount of stress you can handle dictates your reaction to a given situation. Stress has the power to motivate or destroy your performance—and, because stress will always remain in your life, how you handle it is important.

Worry is stressful. All of us spend too much time worrying about things that just might happen. We see all the negatives and live through worst-case scenarios. The answer is to deal with problems as they arise. Don't dwell on the unknown; it's a counter-productive use of your imagination. And for goodness' sake, vent your feelings—or you'll become a time bomb ready to explode!

Stress is not only a personal problem, it's a national issue. The government spends billions through the health care system on the treatment of stress-related problems. Heart disease, obesity, alcoholism, and drugs are a few of the hundreds of mental and physical symptoms manifested by thousands of people. Stress leads to spousal abuse and family breakup. Children can often suffer the same problems, and the cycle repeats itself.

But—wait!—this is a business book, so have I forgotten the topic at hand? I don't think so. For instance, how far can you push an employee before you suffer a loss of productivity? What part does stress play in accidents, absenteeism, and poor work performance? When stress controls a situation, it is emotion, not logic, that takes over, and anything can happen. The wise boss will try to create a safety valve to reduce this tension and help heal, not increase, the pain.

I read a book recently which said the only people without problems are in the graveyard. Truer words were never spoken. We must learn to monitor our own stress levels and try to understand the emotions involved. We must learn to control and increase the amount of stress we can handle. *Don't try to avoid stressful situations; try to manage them.*

Many people use exercise as a stress reducer. When the body works hard, it relaxes the mind. Others like to meditate or pray because they find it helps them place things in perspective. I personally prefer a hot bath and a good book. It can do wonders. Some people turn to hobbies or volunteer work, others join groups or clubs, while still others watch TV. The list is endless. Tears are also a good antidote to stress or anxiety, and we shouldn't be afraid to let them flow. The important point is to find a *healthy* way to relieve your tension. Forget cigarettes, the bottle or drugs and go for a walk! It's time to experience a "reality trip".

Here is a little personal formula I use to help myself control stress.

S   stop
T   trying to
R   rush, rate, run or rationalize
E   every
S   single
S   situation

You Don't Know My Employees!

RIGHT ABOUT NOW, you might be asking how I can presume to offer suggestions about your business when I don't even know your particular situation. How can I understand your organization, your employees, or the people you deal with every day? Obviously, I can't directly, but, as a fellow human being, I *can* relate to your emotional responses. You're not alone in experiencing frustration, stress, hurt or anger. And I understand how it feels to reach that fork in the road, wondering if your responsibilities have grown out of proportion...worrying if you have the right to judge others...concerned that your expectations of your employees are too high...

This book acknowledges these concerns. I know what it feels like when your stomach knots up...when your work has lost its challenge. And how it isn't just one situation that has hurt, but many small incidents, each one almost too insignificant to mention, which have cumulatively attacked and diminished your performance.

In life, we are never going to see eye to eye with everyone. There will be people we can easily relate to, and others with whom it's a real chore! So, part of being a mature individual is to balance and understand other points of view. Recognize that all personalities differ—and always try to respond with the same kind and civil attitude. You'll find the effort reduces your own stress and vastly improves business relationships.

Equally important: *don't be too hard on yourself.* We know you're the best qualified for the job—but we don't expect you to be some kind of saint or super hero. You're simply another human being performing a leadership role—neither better nor worse than anyone else. You have been given a degree of power, and it's up to you how you use it. Remember, though, that you'll be more effective if you enlist the willing support of your employees. They can't control your behavior, but they *can* decide how much they will allow you to affect their personal performance. Their attitude, in fact, can be the deciding factor in your success or lack of it. Ultimately, they decide who is to be respected or disrespected.

Have you ever enjoyed a job? If your answer is "No", maybe the problem isn't your employer or your employees. Perhaps it's time to examine your attitude toward work more closely. You may be the one who needs to make changes. Work isn't something you should always dislike. The tasks may change, the companies may differ, but if you always focus on the negative aspects of your job, you'll never be content. Your employees will reflect your negative attitude. If all your past jobs have brought grievances and irritation and seemed to lead to a dead end, the dissatisfaction could be of your own making. You may be *fighting* work, and no matter how often you change jobs, the problems are likely to continue.

If you're sure your problems don't stem from your attitude, then look long and hard at the individuals or situations that caused them. Never ignore or trivialize problems. If something is hampering your performance or diminishing your job satisfaction, then it should be resolved.

Anger Will Not Help You Accomplish Your Objective; It Will Only Hamper Your Progress.

Add Humor, Have Fun

BUSINESS HAS NO TIME FOR JOKES. We don't get paid to be funny. Humor destroys the corporate image. We are true professionals when we can hold back a grin and become as starchy as our suits. Fun is reserved for our time off. We can't be doing a good job if we enjoy our work.

Needless to say, the entire preceding paragraph couldn't be farther from the truth! Whether we admit it or not, laughter, humor and fun play an important role in business. They relieve pressure, soften the blows, and maintain our humanity in what can be a cold and impersonal marketplace.

The happiest and most successful people I know are those who truly enjoy what they do and who can laugh at a trying situation. *They recognize that life can be very serious, but they also know that fulfillment comes to the person who can see the sun even when it's behind the clouds.*

People will devote a lot of energy to something they find rewarding, so when jobs are enjoyable, the company benefits. If you place a new cartoon on the bulletin board or your secretary finds a joke as she opens a file, you're doing more than breaking the monotony; you're injecting enthusiasm.

Having fun can become very infectious and it doesn't take long for others to come down with the symptoms. We all like to be surrounded by positive, happy people.

Customers love to share your enjoyment. And you don't have to be silly or tell corny jokes to get their attention…merely include them in your good times. They like to be singled out and to know their presence is appreciated. If you feel comfortable enough to share your feelings with them, you'll find they'll react positively. You'll lose your cardboard image, and they'll see the *person* instead of the worker. In particular, restaurants and other such ventures in the service industry can make business flourish with this kind of personal attention.

Stressful situations become more manageable when people add a pinch of humor. When all else fails, an appeal to our lighter side can resolve seemingly impossible problems. Nothing beats these "twinkle-in-the-eye" or "people-pleaser" solutions.

I once worked at a job where the customers had to fill in forms all the time. The employees were always complaining about people walking away with their pens. I found an easy solution! I would take two pens to work, then remove the top from the second pen and place it in my pocket. Of course, a pen isn't much good without its top. When I gave it out, I would smile and tell the customer it was my pet pen and to please return it. The customer would laugh and usually remember to bring it back. *Mind you, if you happen to find any lost pet pens that have flipped their lids, they probably belong to me!*

He Has Achieved Success Who Has Lived Well, Laughed Often, And Loved Much.
Unknown

Customer Service:
A Byproduct

THE NINETIES ARE HERE, and everywhere you look, companies are rediscovering service. As consumption has declined, customers have taken on new importance. As the economy has weakened, it's become vital to maintain good relations with customers and clients. Suddenly, it's okay to be nice to people—and while this may seem like a new concept to some, it's a practise every truly successful business has followed for years.

In our global village, competition doesn't only come from the company next door; it can originate from halfway around the world. Clients and customers also come from all corners of the globe. And where products and services are comparable, often the only distinguishing characteristic is the quality of our service.

Corporations invest in customer relations because a satisfied customer is a repeat customer. They research the buying practises of their clients and target their specific market through advertising. They strive to satisfy the desires of customers, based on accumulated data.

Everywhere, businesses are busy creating neat customer service divisions. They train their staff in the new policies. They work to create a customer-friendly environment. But while the ideas and concepts are well-meant and offer much useful information, *they all miss one important step.*

Customer service is a byproduct and will be consistently successful only if the employees enjoy their jobs, and suffer minimal stress. Customers can sense the mood of a business, and this will be the biggest single factor in their decision whether or not to return.

What would happen if a hockey team's executives were

interested only in the fans? They could improve the stadiums with more comfortable seats, create better ice conditions, and introduce many enjoyable extras for the spectators. They might even get new equipment and designer uniforms for the players. But if management failed to show concern for the team, the players would lack a bond with each other and no one would feel like a vital contributor to the club's performance. The players' talents would be squandered, because they would have had no proper training. In spite of the beautiful surroundings, the fans would soon become disinterested and stop coming to the games.

It is team spirit that creates the "magic" that fans come to watch. A good hockey club knows that the players are the most important element in its success. They are the basis of a winning organization.

Business is no different. The employees become the company in the customers' eyes and their attitude makes all the difference in selling your product. So often, it isn't what employees say—*it's how they say it*. People can sense cold, uncaring vibes. Customers will put up their guards, and the trust between business and customer will break down. Customers probably won't say a word; they'll simply take their business elsewhere.

Discover The Power Of Compound Care.

The Biggest Reward—
A Sense Of Accomplishment

HOW WE ALL LOVE TO BE ACKNOWLEDGED...to receive an appreciative pat on the back...to experience a true sense of accomplishment...to feel that rush of adrenaline and pride!

Such personal satisfaction is one of the biggest rewards we can experience, yet the situations which trigger that feeling differ greatly between individuals.

There is no set formula for making someone happy, because we all set our own standards for personal accomplishments. We are all different—and what motivates one person can be a real turnoff to the next.

Some believe that the keys to happiness are wealth, power, and beauty. These assets may well distinguish a successful person, but they are the rewards of having learned an art—not the reasons for individual success. This concept is a bit hard to explain, so I'll try by telling one of my stories.

An inexperienced gardener buys a rosebush and then does some research to find out how much sunlight it needs, what the best soil is, how often it must be watered, and how much fertilizer is needed to make it blossom. He watches over his plant and nurtures it carefully. The appearance of the first bud kindles the gardener's sense of pride, and the resulting blossom is ample reward for the hard work, time, and knowledge spent in growing it. *The gardener could have gone to the florist and paid for a perfect rose, but he could never buy the same feeling of accomplishment.*

When you have developed a workforce that takes personal pride in their accomplishments, then you'll have a successful business. Most people prefer to be members of a winning team, rather than star performers on a losing one. If employees feel they are moving backwards, they will become unmotivated, dissatisfied and stagnant in their performance. On the other hand, if they're given a positive goal, *and are supported with respect and appreciation,* they will perform beyond all expectation.

Effective communication is the single, most important key. You must learn to listen—instead of assuming you know all the answers. One person's measure of accomplishment can't always be judged by others. How we view ourselves can be very different from how others see us. You might be satisfied with an employee's performance, but if the employee isn't personally satisfied with his or her own work, your company will lose.

Sometimes a small pat on the back can provide a great deal of support. Appreciation is often a bigger motivator than a paycheck.

A Paycheck Feeds The Bank Account; Appreciation Feeds The Soul.

The Labor Union:
Backbone Or Crutch?

IF YOU EVER WANT TO GET A GROUP of people into a heated discussion, ask their opinions of labor unions. Everyone has a list of pros and cons to justify their personal beliefs on this subject. People love to hate them or hate to love them. Yet many agree that unions are largely responsible for the way in which the workforce has developed over the last century. By initiating social reform, they have ensured their place in history.

I think the first thing we must remember about unions is that *they don't usually choose their members.* The company hires a worker and that person then becomes a member of the representing union. In effect, your business has control of the membership through the individuals it hires.

No matter how it's perceived, a union, in reality, is no more than a united group of employees trying to create better working conditions and standards. Unlike business executives who are assigned positions, union leaders are voted in by a democratic process. The membership has the right to terminate their service or extend it. These elected individuals are only representing the opinion of the majority of union members.

Unions can take credit for having developed a higher standard of living around the world. They helped create a stronger middle class in society, greatly improving the financial and personal well-being of millions of people. Medical, dental, insurance and pension programs have all been enhanced by the union movement. It's true that non-union companies also have these plans, but often they are only implemented to keep pace with their unionized counterparts. Unions provide a balance between the rich getting richer and the poor getting poorer. In some ways, they are the Robin Hoods of the modern-day world.

One thing unions do is eliminate many of the gray areas that have characterized business. To a large extent, the rules are reduced to simple black and white—and both sides benefit. It's like a common board game where the rules are clearly spelled out for all participants. If a problem arises, you check the rulebook. Of course, any rule can be changed if all parties agree—because even common standards need a certain amount of flexibility to respond to individual circumstances. Business and unions lock horns when one or both parties become rigid and inflexible in their beliefs.

But in spite of the good accomplished by unions, there are some problems. For example, a couple of areas that concern me about union policy are the common wage scale and the protection of the lazy employee. Can membership in a union diminish the ambition of some individual members?

Unions and businesses should not see themselves as rivals but as team players dedicated to forging a better and more caring labor force. The emphasis should not be on competition, but on cooperation. *I believe companies and unions will need to refocus in the coming years and work more closely together. Intimidation and misunderstanding will hamper progress, not enhance it. Unions can, and will, have a place—but they must recognize reality and change with the times.*

The Voice Of Unions Can Enrich The Corporate Song.

Strikes:
Labor Lashing Out

A STRIKE SHOULD ONLY BE THE TACTIC OF LAST RESORT in an extreme situation. It is the equivalent of labor going to war, and the outcome is always characterized by bitterness, hurt and mistrust. I don't believe there is ever a clear winner. A strike only places people in conflict, thereby creating divisiveness within a company.

Adopting peaceful methods of settling disputes should not be seen as a weakness. Sometimes, non-threatening dialogue can move each side to a better understanding of the other's position. Differences of opinion can be aired without anger exacerbating the problem.

People will fight back if they feel they have been backed into a corner with no means of escape. Ask the same people for a fair compromise, and quite possibly a stronger, more productive relationship will develop. At worst, you'll know that you tried your best by attempting to defuse the situation in a mature fashion.

Who suffers from a strike? I see three losers: the company, the employees, and the people who are directly affected by the breakdown of service. The only winners are the media, who seem to love wallowing in the misfortunes of others. Strikes sell papers and increase ratings, but do nothing to rectify situations. In fact, they can aggravate them.

My heart goes out to those on strike, for they aren't bad or greedy people—merely individuals caught up in an unfortunate situation. Sure, you'll always find a few who become militant and use a strike as an excuse to break the law, but they're the exception.

Sometimes, the biggest problems come from negotiating committees, who remind me of a group playing strip poker. Opposing sides go in wearing ten or more outfits, and through the course of the game they shed several layers, each reporting on the other's losses. As they get down to the last few layers, the game becomes more intense and they begin to take their positions more seriously. The game inevitably ends with all parties leaving the table fully clothed and comfortable. It's a ritual in which everyone is expected to drop some of the excess attire, for their wants and needs have been exaggerated just so they can play the game effectively.

But whatever happened to honest, caring communication and good faith negotiations? *Game playing should not be used when other people must pay the price.*

Unions should never be expected to roll over and play dead, but neither should they have their heads in the clouds if they are to function in today's business world.

People, Productivity, And Profits Must Be The Prime Concerns Of Both Parties.

Women *Can* Be Themselves
And Succeed

IS THERE REALLY AN INVISIBLE BARRIER called "the glass ceiling"? How far have women progressed in the last couple of generations? Can women compare their achievements to those of their male counterparts?

Women have faced a very tough challenge in past decades, and they have made significant progress in a number of key areas. But while many doors have been opened, more remain closed. In the contemporary workplace, women must still prove themselves to men as worthy competitors. When I hear women protesting, "WHY?" and "IT'S NOT FAIR!", I tend to agree. However, I also know that changes seldom happen overnight and life is not always fair. In facing the challenges that lie ahead, the secret is strategy with patience. Speaking as a woman, I hope we can play the game fairly and demonstrate our honesty, sincerity and determination. If we give way to frustration, anger or mistrust, we will all lose in the long run.

The sexes are not going to change; there will always be male and female. What *can* change is our respective attitudes. I believe we're here to complement each other, not compete. In doing so, we can learn to appreciate our differences. Women can and will accomplish great things, but we will have to marshal our energy, determination and willpower. We must find motivation from within and from one another—not merely through formal external support, such as government legislation.

I know a woman who went from a bright legal career into politics and became very successful. She once gave a speech in which she acknowledged there was a "glass ceiling", but it was something she had never had to deal with personally. Talking with her afterwards, I suggested that she might have realized it was there but had never let it stop her. With a twinkle in her eye, she conceded that I had made a valid point.

I'm a firm believer in hard work. I think satisfying work is essential to personal fulfillment. Work stimulates the mind and creates happy individuals. Lazy people give little and get even less in return. If a job is easy to obtain, it sometimes isn't taken seriously. The rewards lie partly in the journey and not solely in the final destination. Women might have to work harder at reaching their goals, but they will have experienced much growth and understanding in the process.

A man and a woman were traveling separately to a city five hundred miles away. The man had the opportunity to drive the freeway in an air-conditioned car. The woman, however, had to take a much older, unreliable car, and her trip took her over dusty back-roads. The man traveled in comfort and arrived at his destination early. His trip was uneventful. The woman's car broke down but she met a nice elderly man who helped her fix it. She traveled slowly, taking the time to gaze at the lovely scenery, and to enjoy the warm sun through the window. She had to slow down a few times to let cows cross, and once was almost run off the road by a man driving much too fast. At one point, she was delayed by a fallen tree, and it took several fellow travelers working together to move the obstacle out of the way. The group shared the hard work, but also enjoyed many laughs as they completed the job. Did she ever reach her destination? That's up to you to decide. *But who had the more rewarding journey?*

Women are equal to men, but they are very different and they should take pride in that reality. If they try to act like men, they will always fall short. Women have special talents that help them get their work done. Most men appreciate these characteristics, but the few who feel threatened by women will have to deal with their own feelings. Women cannot accept responsibility for this as it is the man's inadequacy, not theirs. They may be slowed by such men but they will never be stopped.

Nuts And Bolts
Serve No Purpose
Unless They Work Together

There Is No Right Or Wrong
To Feelings;
If A Problem Exists,
It Must Be Addressed.

Frustration,
Or Getting Nowhere Fast.

I JUST LOOKED UP "FRUSTRATION" in the dictionary and it says, "to bring to nothing." In my present state of mind, it seems like a most appropriate subject for this section. Let me explain. After a day of writing yesterday, my computer decided to erase itself—with a little help from me. A day's work disappeared down the electronic drain. Technology is wonderful, but I wish it had some common sense.

To say it's been a bad week is an understatement. First off, my printer decided to lose its "e" and all my copies were "e"-less. A sheet of paper without any "e"s looks really funny and it's a little hard to read. Also, my office is the spare room in the basement and it gets pretty cold down there. I probably look like an Eskimo at the keyboard. My husband is very helpful. He tells me it will warm up once winter comes and the furnace kicks in. I guess I'll type in gloves until then. Mitts don't work so well.

You might wonder why I'm recounting such trivial problems here. I'm sure you've experienced similar frustrations. The point, of course, is that the biggest problem lies with me. It's hard for all of us to always remain self-motivated and to pursue our dreams. In my case, I could use the excuse that the basement is too cold or that I have too many other demands on my time. The fact is, if I quit, I would only be cheating myself.

Like any enterprise, a business comes with its share of frustrations. Your employees can be late, call in sick when you need them most, or quit without notice. Customer accounts can be in arrears, and the cash flow as low as your morale. You might tend to feel as if you have all your fingers in the dike, while the dam continues to spring leaks all around you.

Frustration is part of normal living. It's a test of our determination. When we recognize frustration as an inevitable hurdle in the course of our lives, it becomes manageable... something we can get over. It is short-sighted to let negative situations create permanent barriers—the walls that turn us away from our original dreams.

We hear much about goal setting and ways of achieving these goals. We are advised to write down what our ambitions are and review them often to give us direction. It's a great idea, but more often than not, our focus is on material achievements, like getting a new car or paying off the mortgage. I think the concept should be taken a step further and we should list and review *purposes*.

A purpose doesn't mean we have to become famous and produce great ideas or inventions, but the direction we choose should help the world in some small way. Our goal might be simply to be a loving parent, a good friend, or a productive volunteer. A purpose demands that we don't only take, but remain willing to give something back. *Frustration can be diminished, even eliminated, by a sense of purpose.*

Make Sure You Treat Yourself Fairly.
It Doesn't Matter What You Do
If You Can Find Peace From Within.

Flexibility Isn't Just
For Athletes

RULES ARE MADE TO BE BROKEN. For the progressive boss, this phrase has a lot of merit. Obviously, certain laws and rules are necessary for business and everyday living. We need standards to help maintain order in our lives. But like everything else, they're only successful if they fulfill their original purpose. Too often, rules become outdated and cause more problems than they solve.

The problem is, we assume rules are cast in stone and we must follow them, "just because". *Red tape* has resulted in countless hours of wasted manpower—time which could have been spent much more productively. Rules should never become company idols, to be blindly accepted and worshipped.

Most companies hold staff meetings on a regular basis, "just because". In my experience, these usually degenerate into little more than social gatherings in which to compare weekend stories and sport scores. *All too often, prearranged meetings are predictable. They have no freshness about them—and seldom inspire original thinking. They can be a terrible waste of time.*

On the other hand, communication is extremely important in business, and meetings can be vital. However, each meeting must have a definite purpose—such as to introduce new faces, encourage new ideas, and reinforce your most effective policies. Such group communication helps your employees gain a better perspective and become more involved.

We've all found ourselves in the following situation. We go into a store with a problem and are confronted by a clerk who can't make a decision. The clerk needs to get the supervisor who, in turn, must get approval from the manager. What started as a small incident now has three people working on it, with no one committed to reaching a solution. Meantime, neglected customers are milling around and you begin to feel you've been dropped into the middle of a three-ring circus. A molehill grows into a mountain.

Customers and clients appreciate getting quick answers. They react negatively when authority figures exhibit mass confusion.

If your business is flexible and your employees are given a broad range of options for making decisions, they will learn to spread their wings and try new approaches. People appreciate being given a sense of freedom, and they become much more creative *if fewer rules are in place.*

If you can eliminate some bureaucracy and concentrate on innovation, it makes life more fun for everyone. Both morale and bottom-line profits will improve accordingly.

We Must Learn To Flex Our Minds And Stretch Our Capabilities.

Be In Control,
But Don't Control

CORPORATE EXECUTIVES MUST KEEP A FINGER ON THE PULSE of their company. They are the ones who establish its personality...who choose the direction in which the business will travel. They must be willing to make unpopular decisions, and be prepared to suffer the consequences of their actions. They must take full control to get the job done properly. Strong management is very important to the success of a business, and employees need to know who's setting the ground rules.

However, if employees have too many bosses, they get mixed signals and don't know to whom they should listen. Their leaders, in turn, feel it necessary to justify *their* positions, and power struggles result. *Make sure your company doesn't have too many bosses trying to control the direction of your business.*

There's an art to the use of authority. Though very much *in* control, the effective boss doesn't need *to* control. It's the difference between guiding a company of people and pushing them. A good leader expects much from the group—but no more than he or she is also prepared to give. As a result, a bond of mutual respect develops, with each person willingly prepared to enhance the other's performance.

On the other hand, a person who *must* control is often motivated by fear and will feel threatened by another's success. Such individuals expect very little from their fellow employees and consequently, that's what they get. These glory seekers love to take credit for the hard work of others—riding on the backs of those more dedicated and giving nothing in return. They usually prey on the weak because it helps them feel stronger. Because everything they do is for personal gain, "controllers" are the parasites of business.

The last paragraph uses strong language, and as I reread it, I wonder how you will react. I like to think of myself as fair, and capable of finding good in everyone. However, anger took over for a minute and my fingers moved by themselves across the keyboard. Maybe it's because I've seen people needlessly hurt by those who mistake control for leadership.

When You Hurt Other People, You Hurt Yourself More.

Professional Doesn't Mean Cold and Stuffy

ONE NICE THING ABOUT THE NINETIES: the "nose in the air" business is as dead as the dodo. Businesses can no longer afford to make customers feel they're doing them a favor by servicing their needs. These days, consumers will walk away from any business that treats them with indifference.

Successful companies portray a professional image, an image that sets them apart from the competition. They follow the mature, intelligent and honest business practises that have always ensured success. But others take their good intentions just a little too far, confusing professionalism with pretentiousness. For these companies, the result is an aloof attitude that often keeps profits at a distance.

When I finished high school, I took a year off before starting college. I moved away from my small town and went to live in the "big city". I was lucky enough to get a job in a large furniture store catering to the wealthy. It had seven floors of fine wood furniture. I had the honor of being the store's youngest salesperson, and I was assigned to lamps and fireplace accessories. Like all the staff, I was expected to wear conventional business colors like black, gray, navy or white. The only person who dressed any differently was the elevator lady: I really envied her bright red jacket! For all their staid behavior, my colleagues were kind and supportive; I suspect because my youth and bubbliness were something of a novelty.

We were all treated well, but I sometimes felt I'd joined the army because we were never allowed to address each other by our first names. We had to treat our customers so formally that our jobs could almost as easily have been done by robots. Being a small town girl, I constantly forgot myself and would smile or crack a joke with the people I was serving. I would immediately sense them letting down their guard and beginning to enjoy themselves. The job was interesting, but I soon felt it was time to quit straightening lampshades and wrapping electrical cords and go back to school.

No business should be intimidating to its customers. By the same token, your staff should never be intimidated by your customers. Intimidation is a form of control, and no one performs well under its yoke. Truly successful people never employ intimidation because it shows weakness, not strength.

You must walk the line between being professional and being yourself. If you act naturally, people will trust you and believe in your honesty and sincerity. You can't be like me and I can't be like you. We have to find our individual comfort zones and work within them. You must believe in who you are and rely on the tools that nature gave *you* and only you. If you try to act like someone else, people will see only a mask and fail to trust the face under it.

You must work within the boundaries of good business practise. Concentrate on being friendly, and use good manners. Integrate these qualities into your own unique package and add your own spark of personality. *Others will be willing to share their feelings with you, if they sense you are sharing yourself with them.*

Here is a story that proves my point nicely. It happened to me a long time ago. I stopped at a grocery store to pick up some last-minute shopping. I had purchased everything on my list except one important item, and I couldn't find it anywhere. I went up to the boy stocking the shelves and asked, "Can you tell me where you keep your shoelaces?" He looked up at me and then, without a word, slowly looked down at his feet. I started to laugh, as this fellow's sense of timing and humor was perfect.

I left the store in a much better mood than when I had entered. He could never have been taught it—but with this simple act, he enhanced the image of his employer in ways that cannot be measured.

Be Yourself.
You Are The Only One
Who Can Deliver
Your Message.

Do You Know
What's Expected Of You?

WE ALL HAVE A PRETTY GOOD IDEA of our particular job function. But it's important to make sure that our aims and expectations are shared by our employer and our superiors. A football team can have all the talent in the world—but if the coaching staff doesn't assign individual responsibilities, the team won't win many games. The players can't perform at their best with only a partial understanding of their roles in the strategy of the game. They must understand completely to excel at their positions.

Many people feel silly asking the boss what's expected of them. They may have worked in the same position for years, yet still be unsure how their superiors measure their performance. Sometimes, they answer to several individuals and each of these under-bosses has a different idea what the person's work entails. There are too many orders coming from too many directions.

To perform most effectively, everyone needs a job description. No one wants to ask repeatedly, "What should I do next?" or "How do you do that?" When you make your expectations clear, your staff understands their responsibilities and learns to work independently. *Communicate. Communicate. Communicate.*

Without set guidelines, it's not uncommon to see several people duplicating work while other work is being ignored. Productivity declines—as excessive time, energy and intellect is expended without corresponding results. As a manager, you don't need to hear excuses like, "I thought it was his job," or, "We both were looking into it!" Duplication is like two people washing the laundry and no one drying it! The job never gets finished, and your clothes become mildewed.

A job description doesn't always need to be cast in stone. It can be changed, but it must be fully understood by the person responsible as well as by everyone else involved in the project. Mindreading doesn't work well in the office.

If You Think You Know Everything, You Might Have Much To Learn.

Our Souls Are Nurtured
By The Care
We Give And Receive.

The 'R'uins Of Business

HERE ARE SOME HAZARDS I believe can cause the downfall of any good company.

RUMORS Rumors have a propensity to grow big and fast. It would be wonderful if your money could compound as quickly as a rumor and take on so much interest. Rumors can destroy both companies and individuals. They should never be dismissed as insignificant. *Keep your staff informed.* Don't ever be secretive, or you will plant the seeds of rumor. Give your employees both the bad and the good news that concerns them, and don't leave hints of impending developments to be misshapen by an overactive imagination. Don't think any rumor will die a quick death on its own. Rumors create mistrust, fear and misunderstanding. Make sure your staff and customers know the difference between fact and fiction.

ROMANCE This issue is one real hot topic. How do we learn to separate our professional and private lives? We have to take our hormones to the office with us, and they sure can cause a lot of problems! You have only to read Ann Landers or Dear Abby to realize that *office romance is alive and well and wreaking havoc.* The damage it can do is incalculable. Many bright careers have been extinguished because of office relationships. I believe your willpower must be stronger than your passion power. Make sure your eyes are wide open if you begin a relationship with a co-worker, and be ready to suffer the consequences!

RUDENESS Rude people are conductors of negativity. They disrupt the flow of a business and drain its energy. Respect is important to people, and rudeness destroys it. I can tolerate almost anything, but my fuse is very short when someone is rude. I believe a *heavy* hand should be brought down on people who use insulting behavior to control others.

RIDICULE Too much time in business is spent finding fault with others when it could be used more productively to focus on our own shortcomings. When the workplace becomes a battleground for personal mudslinging, many brilliant ideas and careers are left in the dirt.

RUNNING Many companies have a habit of over-running everything: their budgets, their time, their expectations. *Running* a business is different from *guiding* one. People lose their creativity if they feel they are being controlled. If your company has an operations manual, make sure it allows for some flexibility and individuality.

REALITY What has worked in the past might not work today or in the future. Be ready to change with the times. Don't just try to find answers to old questions. Look for new questions, and answer them imaginatively.

Clean And Paint

THIS BOOK IS BASED MOSTLY ON FEELINGS, but I think it's also appropriate to talk briefly about the practical approach to business. That's because your presentation is every bit as important as your personality. You only have one chance to make a first impression. Customers are quick to judge and very slow to change their minds if a business doesn't meet their expectations.

Depending on your nature, you might get used to a mess in your office or to a burned-out light bulb on your sign. Such small everyday details may be given low priority when you're concerned with more important decisions. Unfortunately, that burned-out bulb is often the first thing customers notice and it reflects instantly on how your business is judged.

I'm certainly not suggesting that you install potted plants by the welding machines, or spend thousands of dollars designing your front offices. When it's clean, neat and well-organized, your business presents an image that's appealing without being expensive. On the other hand, you can display the most beautiful pair of drapes, but if they're grubby and have hooks missing, they will detract from the appearance of your establishment. Add these to a dirty window and the effect is terrible! Outward appearance has much to do with the way your business is perceived and nothing polishes up your image like a little elbow grease.

Here's one example we can all relate to. Every one of us has had occasion to use the washrooms in different businesses and venues—and conditions, as you know, can vary from hygienic to downright disgusting. Sometimes it looks as if the washroom gets one cleaning a year, and it's already been overdue for six months. Ask yourself: is this how you want your organization to be remembered?

The outward appearance of your business conveys your pride

or lack of it, and your employees won't maintain any higher standards than the business does itself. If your lunchroom has dirty walls, cluttered tables, and old magazines lying around, users will rarely accept any responsibility for cleaning up. Without direction, they'll usually leave it the way they found it—and the mess won't get any better, just worse.

Cleanliness and personal presentation are areas in which you can lead by example. When you are consistently well-groomed, you promote a similar pride among your staff. On the other hand, if you come in looking like an unmade bed, how can you expect anything better from your personnel? Personal hygiene is particularly important. If the work is dirty, why not provide shower and laundry facilities? Ensure that towels are replaced and coveralls are washed daily. Individuals who are clean and neat feel better about themselves and their company.

Take a critical look around your establishment and see what you can do to make it more appealing. This might include picking up garbage in the parking lot, cutting grass, sweeping sidewalks, or making sure your premises are bright and well-lit. Inside, the workplace should be clean, organized, and well treated. An organized desk gives a far better impression than a cluttered workplace with papers scattered around. Dirty ashtrays and day-old coffee mugs should not be left out for all to see.

Make the cleanup fun. You might designate the last hour every Friday and have everyone pitch in. Ask for suggestions on how to improve the workplace, and make the cleanup a team effort. Your employees will get a chance to do something other than their daily routine and they'll end the week with a sense of accomplishment. On Monday mornings, they'll be greeted with neat surroundings—a stimulating way to start a new week.

Once or twice a year, hold a Clean-a-thon. Take a weekend and have the employees and their families come and do the painting, fix-ups and spring or fall cleaning. Throw a large family barbecue or party afterwards hosted by the company. Instead of paying the employees, give the money earned to a charity of their choice. Everyone wins. The company gets a needed facelift, the employees improve their workplace, their families share in the fun and the charity gets a cash donation. If you don't like this idea, make up one of your own or encourage suggestions matched to your particular needs.

Soap, Water, And Paint Have Magical Powers.

Do You Use Your Shoe As A Hammer?

IT WAS A SMART PERSON who invented masking tape. I'm sure my first apartment would have fallen apart without it. That was in my younger, single days when my toolbox consisted of a shoe for a hammer, the end of a knife for a screwdriver, and lots and lots of masking tape. I even remember the time I fixed my toilet with the stuff! Thank goodness I married a man who brought a *real* toolbox into the marriage.

Many businesses get by with inadequate equipment. When it breaks down, this causes unnecessary stress on employees and many lost hours of productivity. The cost of downtime alone demands that equipment be well maintained and in good working order. The best butcher has a sharp knife. The most effective secretary uses a typewriter or computer that functions well. Train your staff on their equipment, and show them how to do basic repairs and upkeep. Don't wait till it's broken; fix it first. Your company can lose a great deal if vital equipment breaks down and needs to be replaced.

Most businesses keep a first aid kit handy, so they can mend cut fingers and take care of minor health problems. But your machinery also needs a first aid kit in the form of a toolbox. In the efficient workplace, nails are not hammered with a shoe. (I remember breaking many a ballpoint pen trying to unjam a clogged printer. It certainly didn't do my pens any good and I'm sure it wasn't good for the printer, either!) Most of us work on high-tech equipment, and it's essential that we have some training on the do's and don'ts of these machines.

For the sake of your sanity, make sure repairs are done when needed and don't resort to temporary fixes on a make-do program.

There's just not enough masking tape in the world. Have someone make a list of needed repairs and get them done before minor problems become major. You don't wait for a toothache before you brush your teeth, do you?

Keeping Up Equipment
Will Keep Up
Your Profits.

Incentives For All

I ONCE HEARD OF A COMPANY that provides each employee with a garden plot in which to grow vegetables and flowers. What a wonderful idea! Not only does it show a commitment to the environment, but it gives employees a hobby where there is also an opportunity for accomplishment. Employees are encouraged to enjoy fresh air and exercise, and spend quality time with their families. Better still, people are able to relate differently than they do in the office. Can you imagine comparing *your* tomatoes with those grown by your employees?

The incentives provided by caring companies vary from the expected to the extraordinary. Some businesses have profit-sharing plans or bonuses. Others provide flex hours or gymnasium facilities. Some give extra attention to birthdays and holidays. Still others offer daycare, free courses, extra time off or discounted lunches. The list goes on and on.

What do these incentives accomplish? Are they important and how do companies benefit? Don't employees start to take incentives for granted and start to demand more? Aren't such motivational benefits costly in both time and money?

These are all fair questions that need to be addressed. But I think *the spirit in which incentives are given is the key.* Ask yourself: are you providing extras only because the competition does so—or out of a true sense of care and appreciation? Do you reward your staff without first *finding out what they want?* Do you expect more from your employees with the introduction of incentives, or do you give expecting nothing in return? Is your incentive a sop intended to *pacify,* or a gift meant to *enrich?* Do you constantly tell employees how fortunate they are, or do *you* feel like the lucky one? Do you use these extras as something that can be taken away if your people don't perform well? Do some individuals get more than others?

Is It A Carrot Dangling
In Front Of Them Or
A Sugar Cube Rewarding
A Job Well Done?

Don't Measure Everyone
With The Same Yardstick

SOMETIMES, WE'RE SO BUSY trying to get organized that we can't spare the time to get down to business. Organization—whatever *that* is—has almost become a cult. Society insists on placing people in neatly ordered groups like livestock or vegetables. We're measured, numbered and compared from the time we're born to the time we call it quits. And statistics and data are collected on everything—from our average sock size to our taste in fast foods. Our very existence seems to hinge on numbers.

Sure, measurements and classifications are important. They generate useful data which also provides an unbiased view of history and gives us valuable insight into the future. Used correctly, this data can make a positive difference to our lives.

Sometimes, however, the act of measuring seems to supersede its purpose—like selecting a guard dog strictly by size rather than intelligence and courage. When corporations monitor and measure business and staff performances, they seek to establish a gauge by which to judge the success of the company. But the important word here is "gauge." *Because numbers can be deceptive, they should never be accepted without question, and certainly should not be used to make assumptions about the workforce without any supporting personal communication.*

How many business meetings only review statistics and never address the human side of a company? If ninety percent of your group feels one way, does it mean the ten percent who disagree are wrong, that their views are unimportant and not worth examining?

The problem with judging individuals in accordance with numeric standards is that people quickly learn that they need only live up to the specific set standards. The motivation isn't there to imagine, create and improve. Many won't feel any need to accomplish and excel.

We are all handicapped to a degree. Everyone has areas of weakness. Personally, I'm a rotten speller who has never completely grasped the concept of phonics. But I've never let this deter me from expressing myself. I find that, with practise and a good dictionary, I can formulate my ideas. My husband does a lot of my corrections and I hear him laughing...often! Similarly, he finds math concepts difficult and I'm a whiz with numbers. In business, as in life, you must create a balance and focus on eliminating the weaknesses and enhancing positive talents.

When monitoring employees on the job, let them explain the factors that increase or decrease their performance levels. If you are casting judgment, make sure you have the facts and that the people involved have time to express their views.

Often, when one person reviews another's work performance, the personal view of the reviewer plays a more important role than the task itself. Someone's progress can be halted because of a superior's entrenched views, personal acceptance of the worker...even downright envy. In the process, a business can lose one of its biggest resources—a bright, productive employee.

We've all heard about the half glass of water. The optimist will say it's half full; the pessimist will say it's half empty. Statistics can be interpreted in the same way, and the outlook of the user can affect the way in which they are read.

Place The Papers In The File,
And Replace Them With A Smile.

To Judge
Or Not To Judge?

IN THIS MORNING'S PAPER, there was an advertisement from a company explaining how "customer service-oriented" they have become. They promised to treat people like "kings and queens."

I really have a problem with such statements, for surely it's not up to businesses to judge themselves. This ad reminds me of a gorgeous schoolmate of mine who never tired of telling everyone how attractive she was. We all watched her carefully to see if we could find anything wrong; a pimple, even a hair out of place, was enough. She lost part of her beauty the moment she told others she was beautiful.

Effective people or businesses don't need to tell others how successful they are. When you judge yourself too highly, you aren't leaving any room for improvement, error, or appreciation by others.

Neither your customers nor your employees want to deal with egotism and attitudes of superiority.

It's far better to ask your customers what *they* think, and judge your business performance by their response. I like to be asked my opinions on the quality of service at any place I shop because it adds a human touch. For example, as I was picking up my drycleaning last week, the owner came out and asked how I liked his people's work and how he might provide better service. I was very impressed. He has earned my repeat business.

In the same way, many restaurants and stores invite our opinions through customer comment forms. This is a good concept; it lets us know management is interested in us, and providing better service.

Great bosses don't rate their own performance nor that of

the competition. They believe in firm action, not in empty words. Facts are gathered and the fluff is discarded. They're proud of their accomplishments, but won't disparage the success of others.

I Don't Want To Be Treated
Like A King Or Queen,
But I Do Want To Be Treated
Like A Valuable Individual.

Never Cover The Hole
That Is Dug

I RECENTLY MET A MAN who was most concerned over his company's poor morale and decreased productivity. A feeling of helplessness permeated everything he said. This fellow sincerely wanted to help turn his company around, but he felt that so much damage had already been done, it would take years just to bring things back to square one. The staff had lost so much faith in management, it would take a miracle for them to accept the company as a caring employer.

I quickly saw that, instead of building trust and honor, the management of this company had destroyed these two main ingredients of success. The business had dug itself into a hole and now, even caring employees couldn't see any way out.

But what my friend overlooked was that it really wasn't too late. Acting on personal conviction, he himself could be instrumental in speeding up the healing process. *People who have experienced hurt and disappointment often become stronger individuals.* They know what they don't like about their situations. By this time, his boss certainly had a good understanding of what *didn't* motivate, so there was a great opportunity to find what *would* encourage my friend and his fellow employees.

Past errors can't be undone, but they're an effective learning experience. If you bake a cake that doesn't turn out, you don't swear never to bake another. You analyze the problem and try not to repeat your mistakes. If your cake didn't cook long enough, you bake it longer the next time, but you don't alter the amount of flour. If the recipe itself turns out to be the problem, you don't use it again. A quality cake is the final objective, so work toward that goal. Don't be overwhelmed by minor problems.

Companies are like people. They can be strengthened by adversity or they can let it destroy them. Attitudes determine success or failure.

When a contractor plans to build a house, he knows he must first dig a hole to establish a strong foundation. He could omit this step and still create a wonderful, eye-pleasing structure that, from a distance, would look exactly the same. But this building might not weather the first storm, and it certainly wouldn't age well, having no solid base to support it. Companies that have dug themselves into unproductive holes shouldn't try to cover them up. They should use these holes as the base for a strong foundation—a foundation on which to build lasting businesses.

Solid structures cannot be erected overnight, and cementing them together takes a lot of work and know-how. Concrete is not composed of boulders. Rather, it consists of many small rocks joined together to create strength.

A Situation Is Never Hopeless Unless You Believe It Is.

Letting Go

ONE OF THE HARDEST THINGS a boss must do is tell an employee that his or her services are no longer required. It's an emotional time both for the person being terminated and the individual delivering the bad news. This is one of those stressful, negative situations no one wants to be involved in...part of the dirty work of being a boss. But when a person is hired to do a job, the employer doesn't have a one hundred percent guarantee that the individual is suitable or that he or she will last forever.

Because there are two kinds of termination, I've divided this chapter to address both situations. Though both scenarios lead to the same result, each has a very different solution.

THE EMPLOYEE IS TERMINATED BECAUSE OF UNSUITABLE WORK HABITS.

Let's first discuss the person who is terminated because of unsuitable work habits. I think this problem can be minimized by giving more time and effort to the initial hiring process. By thorough examination, weaknesses can often be detected before a person is ever hired.

The training period is also important, since it shows how well new employees adjust to the assigned work tasks. Are they positive about the learning process? Do they listen and follow instructions? Do they fit in well with the other personnel? These are all areas of concern, since industry needs team players who are adaptable to change and willing to learn.

The first six months in a job is the honeymoon period. The employee will be adjusting to the new work, having had no time to become unmotivated by any prevailing low morale. His or her personality, attitude, and work habits will gradually become more visible, and easy to monitor. If you see a problem developing, *now* is the time to address it decisively. Overlooking the situation will only magnify the problem, not alleviate it. Talk to the employee and be honest, but remember to *attack the problem area* and *not* him or her personally. Comment on the positive aspects of the work performance, and try to agree on solutions regarding the weaker areas. "It seems you're taking one step forward and then two steps backward. I really appreciate the step forward, but how do you think we can make the other two steps move in the same positive direction?"

Effective people *earn* their jobs. They never accept employment as their *right*. Companies should not take their employees for granted, but the employees shouldn't take the company for granted either. Business is a relationship and it takes two willing partners to make it work. It doesn't matter if an employee has worked ten days or twenty-five years, he or she is being paid for productivity and must deliver it every day.

One bad apple can spoil a whole barrel, so make sure it's removed before it does permanent damage. Everyone deserves a chance, but they must also have the personal desire to adapt to their surroundings. Terminating an undesirable employee helps create fairness and contentment on the work floor.

THE EMPLOYEE IS TERMINATED BECAUSE OF LACK OF WORK.

Now, what about employees who are let go because of lack of work? They have served their company well, and now, due to uncontrollable circumstances, they must be terminated. Downsizing has become a way of life in the Nineties and more and more people are finding their positions voided.

This is a delicate situation, and one that needs to be handled with the utmost care. The affected individual feels cast out from the work family and faces an unknown future. He or she questions his or her importance, and often takes termination as a personal failure, worrying how they will manage personally and financially.

In this situation, it's essential that you explain the reasons for terminating the position and do everything in your power to ease the transition for your employee. If possible, you should provide counseling about retraining, the refinement of job-finding skills, and financial management. And don't hesitate to express your sense of loss in parting with a valued contributor. The position might be terminated, but try not to take your former employee's self-image with it.

I once worked for a company that hired seasonal summer employees. Our manager was a quiet man who had a very hard time expressing his feelings. Every September, he would place the temporary employees' termination letters in their mail slots but he never took the opportunity to talk with them personally. He was perceived as cold and impersonal but I believe the opposite was true. I think he found this job so difficult that he avoided it, thus sending out all the wrong signals.

Your commitment as a former employer should not stop with the final paycheck. An accompanying letter or phone call means so much. It gives your former employee encouragement and the assurance that you really do care. Once someone has found a new direction, *then* comes the time to say goodbye.

Whatever the reasons for a termination, it's important to remember you are dealing with a *person—not a commodity*. If we want to build a strong workforce, we must never destroy the worker.

Termination Isn't Only An End – It Is Also A Beginning.

Be A Company
With A Conscience

IS MONEY THE ONLY WAY TO MEASURE SUCCESS? Every business wants to be profitable, because that's what free enterprise is all about. But what is profit? In a way, it's a measure of the contribution every business makes to society. *One of the most effective ways that man can serve others is through profitable enterprise. It's more than just money.*

If companies are only interested in bottom-line results, they begin to lose contact with the marketplace. Quite simply, the marketplace is people. These consumers have an emotional attachment to their money and they will only purchase things whose attractions outweigh this attachment.

Companies must build a foundation of caring and a true vision of what they want to accomplish. A corporation with a conscience and purpose will travel in the right direction. Profits are the measure of that success; they reflect the importance and public acceptance of your products and services. And the people you hire will inevitably determine your company's success or failure. Thus, their concerns must be addressed, and they must be recognized as living, breathing entities. People need to be more than numbers to feel worthy and be productive.

You must first give of yourself before you can ask others to give of themselves. Everyone should share in the success of your company, not just the people who had the initial vision.

Winning businesses stress quality and service, and are active members of the community. They realize they can't take from society without giving something back.

Become a participating member of your community; support clubs, schools, anything that adds to the well-being of the world around you. Don't close yourself off. Come out from behind your corporate desk and throw out the first ball. Then be there to cheer on the rest of your staff as they take to the field. Give of yourself and of your corporate profits.

Try not to always expect something back from your involvement. If your participation is an excuse for free advertising or gaining visibility, then your company has lost sight of its purpose.

I think the important concept here is *balance*. We all know we can't live without money, but we must also take the time to *enjoy* it and *share* it with others.

Life Will Be To A Large Extent What We Ourselves Make It.
Samuel Smiles

Practising
What I Preach

WE ARE ALL TOUCHED BY CERTAIN INDIVIDUALS who have a great impact on our lives. They help us become who we are. They are our support system. Throughout this book, I have stressed the importance of showing appreciation for the help of others. It's a special pleasure, therefore, to acknowledge those much-loved people in my life whose understanding and support made this book possible.

My husband Dave is my mate, best friend, partner and companion. Our relationship is the single most important thing to me. Dave is the man with whom I want to grow old. Successes and failures come and go, but love is something I never want to let die. He believes in me and I in him, and knowing that, we can overcome anything. Out of that love have come two wonderful daughters, Jenny and Carly. They are special children rewarding us with the additional gift of parenthood.

Jenny is fourteen years old and is now taller than I am. She is a kind, energetic teenager, with a tenderness towards others. Jenny is always ready for new challenges and her love for music is only matched by her love of life. Carly is a bright, vivid ten-year-old who generates a warmth toward everyone around her. Her creative abilities are remarkable, and like me, she's a risk-taker. Jenny and Carly share a special bond and respect that I hope will last the rest of their lives. It's an honor to share time with these two children and I'm so proud to be their "Mom."

Allen and Dorothy Thomson have encouraged me along life's journey. I credit the person I am today to them, for they are my parents. Mom and Dad have always set an example worth following. They showed me that life isn't always easy, hard work is healthy, giving doesn't mean receiving, and love isn't something to measure or misuse. These are special people with a special message for others.

True friends are like diamonds—indestructible, precise and rare. Over the past ten years, Monica Brown has been such a friend. Nicky, as she is known by her friends, has the ability to understand and give support. She offers a quality of trust found in very few people. She is like the sister I never had.

Many people have influenced my life. The list is too long to mention names but they are engraved in my memory: my brothers and their families, Dave's Dad and family, the many friends, business and personal acquaintances who have been there over the years for me.

Relationships do not always have to be positive to make an impact. Some of my saddest moments have added to my inner strength. These have helped me understand what I stand for and who I am. Interpersonal relationships are the rewards of life; they give us something no one can ever take away.

Thank You.

Goodbye

MY BOWL JUST RAN OUT of jelly beans. I end this book with tears in my eyes and a lump in my throat—because, in expressing the way I feel, I've learned so much about myself. Those feelings take on new significance when I see them in black and white.

It's now time for you to go in search of your own jelly beans. I wish you success. If you find a new flavor, I urge you to savor it and share it with others. Who knows? By hunting diligently, you might find something important that you didn't even know you were seeking.

This book talks about the human side of business, and what motivates and increases performance in the workplace. I've stressed that you can't change a system without first changing the people within the system. Care, communication, and understanding are fundamental to this effort—but remember, they're only tools with which to accomplish the job. *You* must do the hard work to create the reality. Beautiful, solid relationships take time and patience, but they're worth every ounce of effort. Let's dispense with superficiality, encourage openness and create rock-solid relationships that will weather the test of time.

I've talked about growth and knowledge and how important they are in our personal development. And I want to keep learning. So if *you* come across a jelly bean you would like to share with me, I would love to taste it. Please write, because I would like to get to know you and hear your ideas and comments.

Thank You For Your Time.
And Goodbye Friends.

A Final Story

A WOMAN WAS WALKING THROUGH A PARK ONE DAY when a small bird fell out of its nest. Before she could reach it, a teenage boy had picked it up. She went over to him and asked why he didn't let it go. With a gleam in his eyes he asked, "Is the bird alive or dead?" The woman thought for a moment. She knew that if she said 'dead' he would probably throw the chick away violently. But if she said 'alive', the boy might squeeze the last life out of the creature. She looked at him and calmly said,

"Its fate is in your hands."

Attitude
Is
Everything

About The Author

BORN IN KAMLOOPS, BRITISH COLUMBIA, Janet Andersen was eight years old when her family moved to Fort St. John on the Alaska highway. She fondly recalls the small northern town where *"the temperatures were cold, but the people were warm and caring."* In 1971, she graduated from North Peace High School with the top service and citizenship award.

After exploring city life in Victoria, B.C., she returned to college in Prince George, earning her certificate in Early Childhood Education. In 1974, she joined CP Air as a passenger agent, eventually moving to work with the airline's ticket office in Calgary, Alberta.

Faced with corporate downsizing, she joined Air Canada, Canada's national airline, in 1977. Over the next fourteen years, as an agent at the Calgary airport, she came to epitomize the airline's high standards of service.

In 1989, Janet Andersen was chosen by the Air Canada Hall of Fame for outstanding customer service—the first person chosen from 23,000 employees.

She was asked to be the subject of a video produced by Air Canada which launched a six million dollar program devoted to "Customer Care". The video was shown system-wide.

In 1988, she won the "White Hat" Award, presented by the Calgary Tourist and Convention Bureau for top service in the travel industry category.

Janet Andersen left Air Canada in 1991 and has since formed a company called "Express Appreciation" intended to create the means for companies to show appreciation to their employees and customers.